The First-Time Grantwriter's Guide to Success

This book is dedicated to David DeLoria
and the entire staff of Livonia Central School, Livonia, New York

The First-Time Grantwriter's Guide to Success

Cynthia Knowles

CORWIN PRESS, INC.
A Sage Publications Company
Thousand Oaks, California

For information:

Corwin Press, Inc.
A Sage Publications Company
2455 Teller Road
Thousand Oaks, California 91320
E-mail: order@corwinpress.com

Sage Publications Ltd.
6 Bonhill Street
London EC2A 4PU
United Kingdom

Sage Publications India Pvt. Ltd.
M-32 Market
Greater Kailash I
New Delhi 110 048 India

Printed in the United States of America

Library of Congress Cataloging-in-Publication Data

Knowles, Cynthia R.
  The first-time grantwriter's guide to success / Cynthia Knowles.
      p. cm.
Includes bibliographical references and index.
  ISBN 0-7619-4535-0 (c.: alk. paper)
  ISBN 0-7619-4536-9 (p.: alk. paper)
  1. Educational fund raising-United States-Handbooks, manuals, etc.
2. Proposal writing for grants-United States-Handbooks, manuals,
etc. I. Title.
  LC243.A1 K56 2002
  379.1'2-dc21
                                          2002000155

This book is printed on acid-free paper.

02 03 04 05 10 9 8 7 6 5 4 3 2 1

Acquisitions Editor:	Robb Clouse
Editorial Assistant:	Erin Buchanan
Copy Editor:	Stacey Shimizu
Production Editor:	Denise Santoyo
Typesetter/Designer:	Larry K. Bramble
Indexer:	Molly Hall
Cover Designer:	Tracy E. Miller
Production Artist:	Janet Foulger

Contents

List of Figures

About the Author

Cynthia Knowles is a Prevention Specialist in the field of substance abuse. She previously worked as the Coordinator of the Safe and Drug-Free Schools grant program in the 15-county region of Western New York. She has also worked as a technical reviewer on an ED grant program. She welcomes your feedback, especially your experiences, challenges, insights, and successes with using this guide for grant development. You can contact her at cknowles@localnet.com.

She lives and skis in rural western New York with her husband and son.

Introduction

"How are we going to fund this?" In any organization that is alive with creative ideas, funding is a constant problem. How do you fund new program ideas without cutting back existing services? As school district budgets get voted down or frozen, as the costs for pupil participation in "extra" programs is cut, as staff is trimmed to fit within restricted budgets, there has to be a way of maintaining and even expanding programs. And there is: writing grants. There is grant money available for just about anything if you know where to look and how to write the proposal.

If you are anything like me, the thought of sitting down to write a grant is overwhelming. I finally did it, and so will you. And, believe it or not, you will have success. Maybe not with the first one, but with a little persistence and feedback, you will quickly develop a winning proposal.

Although this guide will focus on the U.S. Department of Education (USDOE) grants and writing to meet their selection criteria, this book remains broadly applicable to assembling *any* grant proposal. We will examine each of the most common selection criteria. Portions of actual grant applications will be included so you can see how the finished product might look.

Throughout the grant process, you will read terms like *authorizing legislation, congressional act, authorizing statute,* and *funding priorities.* The language is very confusing, which is why there is a glossary in the back of this book (see Resource K). As confusing as the jargon can be, take time to understand the authorizing statute as this is key to writing a winning proposal. To fully understand the concept of an authorizing statute requires taking a closer look at where the money for USDOE grant programs comes from. It is a lengthy process, from the allocation of funds in Congress to the awarding of money to a school or agency.

The long and winding road. . . .

All USDOE grant programs begin with an act of Congress. A Congressional Act of this type outlines the purpose and objectives for the proposed grant program. This is called the *authorizing legislation.* Following this act of Congress, the USDOE is then responsible for establishing regulations, or rules, for how this Congressional Act will be carried out. The USDOE develops these rules and sends them to Congress. Congress responds by assigning, or appropriating, funds to this program.

After Congress appropriates funds into a grant program, the responsibility once again goes to the USDOE to develop an application package for the new program and a schedule for awarding funds. Public notice of this new grant program, and the funds that will be available, are published first in the *Federal Register.* This listing will include the requirements for completing an application and the schedule of submission deadlines. This is also called the *Request for Proposals,* or RFP. The *Federal Register* notice is the most complete and most accurate description of the grant program.

The public notice of the grant program in the *Federal Register* will include a program office contact. Call the telephone number provided to receive an application package, which is also called a RFP. This package will include all the forms necessary for making a complete application. Once you complete your application and mail it back to the USDOE, or the specific program office that is coordinating the grant program, it will be officially logged in, screened for completeness, and moved on to the readers. Readers assess, score, and rank order the proposals. Funding recommendations are made, and a final list of award recipients is prepared. The Grants and Contracts Service (GCS) Office will contact each applicant, negotiate final award amounts, and notify Congress of the successful grants.

During the grant period, the Program Office and GCS monitor grants with a combination of annual reports, quarterly budget reports, meetings, trainings that grant recipients are required to attend, and site visits. If you fall out of compliance, the USDOE will work with you to get you back on track so that you can fulfill your proposed plan for programming.

Phew. That's exhausting. Do you still want to do this?

The most critical step in this process is the review of your completed application by the readers. In order to receive an award, the application you submit must receive high scores. In the remainder of this guide, we will walk through each of the most common selection criteria, providing examples and checklists so that your application has a better chance at receiving a high score and subsequent funding.

To simplify this process, there is a glossary at the end of the book, as well as a Frequently Asked Questions (FAQ) section (Resource L). Many of the forms required for submitting a proposal have also been included. There are worksheets and resources to help you write goals and objectives and develop timelines, and chapter checklists to help keep you on track. Flip forward in the book so that you know where everything is.

Who doesn't need the extra money to start that program they have been thinking about. Now is the time to write that grant. The grant you write may create jobs, serve underserved populations, and improve the lives of countless participants. It's worth taking the time to do it well. I hope this guide helps you do that. Let's get started.

Where's the Money? 1

You have undoubtedly heard about colleagues, area schools, and agencies that have received grant money to start up new programs, hire staff, or purchase new equipment. How did they do that? How did they know where the money was and how to apply for it?

There are many sources of information on available money. This chapter will review some primary, secondary, and online sources of funding information, both public and private. You may find that sifting through all of this information to find funding that matches your program needs could become a full-time job. Rather than wonder how colleagues found grant money, you'll be wondering how they narrowed down the field of all the available resources. This will be overwhelming at first.

FUNDING THAT MATCHES NEEDS

Grant programs generally have a particular focus, such as serving an underserved population, expanding a particular program, or examining the generalizability of an established method or program. It helps to understand the funder's intention when trying to find funding that matches your needs.

Program Type

Are you looking for funding to expand a drug prevention program or a science program? If you are planning to expand science programs in your school, then you might want to pay attention to funding opportunities through places like the National Science Foundation. Go to their Website and see if any of their current grant programs match what you have in mind. If, however, you are interested in additional funding for substance abuse programs, then you will want to look at sources of information that summarize just those funding opportunities, such as Websites and newsletters from national organizations, like the Website and electronic newsletter from Join Together or the Substance Abuse Funding News, another newsletter.

Eligibility

Some grant opportunities are only available to nonprofit service providers who can show proof of 501(c)(3) status. Other grants are available only to schools. Some funding is specifically for agencies or community groups. Who is allowed to apply for the funding is called *eligibility*. If the funding looks as if it supports a program or service that your school could use, then partnering with a community agency or nonprofit organization to write the grant together is the way to go.

Population

It is common for funding to target programming to a very specific population, such as students of a particular age or race, or students from a particular socioeconomic group. The funder's goal is to provide more services to this particular group. Do not apply for these funds unless you are planning to serve the specified population.

Results

A grant program may be more relaxed in terms of the population that is served or who is eligible to apply, but they might have very specific results in mind, such as reduced truancy or smoking cessation. The goal of the funder is to discover new ways to deal with the identified problem. These grant programs want to see a wide variety of different, new, and creative methods used to reach these goals.

Techniques

Finally, there are grant programs that want you to use a particular technique to achieve a goal with any population, age, or race. This last grant type is looking for applicability or generalizability of a particular method across a broad population and in different settings.

PRIMARY SOURCES OF FUNDING INFORMATION

There are a few documents and publications that you will want to establish access to because they will contain the bulk of funding information for all federal programs. These are called *primary sources* because they are the direct outlets for information on funding from the federal government.

Federal Register

The *Federal Register* is the federal government's way of informing the public about all new regulations and legal notices issued by federal agencies. This includes authorizing legislation for grant programs. The *Federal Register*, published daily, is the gold standard for information on government funding. Subscriptions are expensive at over $600 a year. Rather than pay for your own subscription, you can access this source for free at most major libraries or colleges.

Catalog of Federal Domestic Assistance (CFDA)

The *Catalog of Federal Domestic Assistance*, also from the federal government, is an annual publication that lists information on all federally funded programs and projects, the distribution of funds, and exactly how to apply for funding. It is available for a much more affordable $70 a year, which includes the current year's volume and all updates. The *CFDA* is also available in most libraries.

Code of Federal Regulations (CFR)

The *Code of Federal Regulations* is an annual document that contains the regulations for all the federal grant programs. You will eventually want to get one of these, because it describes everything you need to know about adhering to all federal grant regulations. This document is broken into so-called Titles, with Title 34 containing the regulations for the U.S. Department of Education (USDOE). If you see a reference to the *CFR* in any publication, it will likely look something like "34 CFR 97(D)," which indicates you should look at Title 34 of the *Code of Federal Regulations*, Part 97, subpart (D). Such a reference tells you exactly where to find the regulation in the *CFR* so that you can examine the regulations if necessary.

Additional primary sources of funding information and information on how to access them are summarized in Figure 1.1.

SECONDARY SOURCES OF FUNDING INFORMATION

Although secondary sources are not as complete as documents like the *Federal Register*, they are much easier to read. These are publications that provide summarized information on grant programs and funding based on information gathered from primary funding sources. Secondary sources are far more accessible and user-friendly than sifting through government publications. Even better, these services are often low or no cost. Many can be accessed on the Internet for free, and others have moderate subscription costs. These can be an excellent starting place for a first-time grantwriter, because most of these secondary information sources are not intimidating. Additional secondary sources of funding information and details on how to access them are summarized in Figure 1.2.

◉ Figure 1.1. Primary Sources of Funding Information

Resource	Mail	Phone
Catalog of Federal Domestic Assistance (CFDA) http://www.cfda.gov/	Superintendent of Documents General Printing Office Washington, DC 20402	202-512-1800
Code of Federal Regulations (CFR) http://www.access.gpo.gov/nara/cfr/cfr-table-search.html	Superintendent of Documents General Printing Office Washington, DC 20402	202-512-1800
Commerce Business Daily http://www.cos.com/	Superintendent of Documents General Printing Office Washington, DC 20402	202-512-1800
Congressional Record http://thomas.loc.gov/	Superintendent of Documents General Printing Office Washington, DC 20402	202-512-1800
Federal Register http://cos.com	Superintendent of Documents General Printing Office Washington, DC 20402	202-512-1800
General Printing Office http://www.access.gpo.gov		
Resources in Education	Superintendent of Documents General Printing Office Washington, DC 20402	202-512-1800
U.S. Government Manual http://www.access.gpo.gov/nara/nara001.html	Superintendent of Documents General Printing Office Washington, DC 20402	202-512-1800

◉ Figure 1.2. Secondary Sources of Funding Information

Resource	Mail	Phone
Annual Register of Grant Support	Order Department Reed Elsevier 121 Chanlon, P.O. Box 31 New Providence, NJ 07974-9904	888-BOWKER2
Chronicle of Higher Education http://www. chronicle.merit.edu/	P.O. Box 1955 Marion, OH 43306-2055	202-466-1032
Education Daily http://www. eddaily.com/	Capitol Publications, Inc. P.O. Box 1453 Alexandria, VA 22314-2053	800-683-4100
Education Week on the Web http://www. edweek.org	Education Funding News 4301 North Fairfax Dr. Suite 875 Arlington, VA 22203	703-528-1082
Federal Grants and Contracts Weekly http://www. eddaily.com	Capitol Publications, Inc. 1101 King Street Alexandria, VA 22314	703-739-6444
Federal Grants Management Handbook http://www. thompson.com/ libraries/ grantsmanage/	Thompson Publishing Group Subscription Service Center P.O. Box 26185 Tampa, FL 33623-6185	800-677-3789
Federal Research Report	951 Pershing Drive Silver Springs, MD 20910-4464	717-872-4230
The Grantsmanship Center	1125 W. Sixth Street Fifth Floor P.O. Box 17220 Los Angeles, CA 90017	213-482-9860
Guide to the Department of Education Programs	Office of Public Affairs U.S. Department of Education 400 Maryland Avenue SW Washington, DC 20202	202-708-8596

Continued

◉ **Figure 1.2.** Continued

Resource	Mail	Phone
Health Grants and Contracts Weekly	Capitol Publications, Inc. P.O. Box 1453 Alexandria, VA 22314-2053	800-826-9972
National Endowment for the Arts Guide to Programs http://arts.endow. gov/learn/	National Endowment for the Arts Public Information Office 1100 Pennsylvania Ave. NE Washington, DC 20506	202-682-5400
National Endowment for the Humanities Overview of Endowment Programs http://www. neh.fed.us	National Endowment for the Humanities 1100 Pennsylvania Ave. SW Washington DC 20506	202-786-0438
National Science Foundation Grant Policy Manual http://www.nsf. gov/home/ grants.htm	Superintendent of Documents General Printing Office Washington, DC 20402	202-512-1800
National Science Foundation E-Bulletin http://www.nsf. gov/home/ ebulletin/	National Science Foundation Washington, DC 20550	
Special Education Report	Capitol Publications, Inc. 1101 King Street Alexandria, VA 22314	800-826-9972
Vocational Training News	Capitol Publications, Inc. 1101 King Street Alexandria, VA 22314	800-826-9972
What Works in Teaching and Learning	Capitol Publications, Inc 1101 King Street Alexandria, VA 22314	800-655-5597

ONLINE SOURCES
OF FUNDING INFORMATION

Internet access has made it easier than ever to locate funding sources. Go to any search engine and type in keywords such as "grants" or "funding." A collection of general grant information collected in this way is displayed in Figure 1.3. Most Websites that report on available grant programs are not intimidating and are easy to navigate.

It is likely that you will read about grant programs and new sources of funding in many other places as well. The *Washington Post,* the *New York Times,* the *Wall Street Journal,* and other national newspapers will often report on congressional activity and the availability of grant money. You might hear something on the TV or radio. Wherever you hear about new appropriations on available federal funding, get the date it happened in congress and refer back to the *Federal Register* for accurate information on the grant program and details on where to send for the application package. The official application notice for any federal grant competition is the one published in the *Federal Register.* As you have seen, grant information may be publicized in other places, but the official, most complete, and most accurate notice will always be found in the *Federal Register.*

PRIVATE, CORPORATE,
AND FOUNDATION FUNDING

Private, corporate, or foundation funding is a little different from federal funding. These are private interests looking for a few good programs to sponsor. Grant awards will vary from very small (a few hundred dollars) to very large (over a million dollars). Grant applications are not always reviewed by a panel of experts, funding decisions are often based on more subjective standards, and applications may not have to adhere to regulations or a format set forth by the USDOE or other federal agency.

A few large volumes summarizing private funding can be found in most libraries. These resources, listed in Figure 1.4, will list all sources of private, corporate, or foundation funding, what they are looking for, and how to make an application to them.

ONLINE GRANTWRITING TOOLS

There are helpful tools on the Internet to help you write and fine-tune your proposal. Take a look at what these sites, listed in Figure 1.5, have to offer to help you with the actual writing.

◉ **Figure 1.3.** Online Sources of Funding Information

Funding Information	Location
Administration for Children and Families (Social Service Block Grants)	http://www.acf.dhhs.gov/
Education Grants	http://www.dir.yahoo.com/ Education/Financial_Aid/Grants/
EduCause	http://www.educause.edu/
The Foundation Center	http://www.fdncenter.org
Grants Information Center	http://www.library.wisc.edu/ libraries/Memorial/grantshp.htm
Grantselect	http://www.grantselect.com/
The Grantsmanship Center	http://www.tgci.com/
GrantsWeb	http://www.research.sunysb.edu/ research/Kirby.html
Healthy Youth Funding Database	http://www2.cdc.gov/nccdphp/ shpfp/index.asp
Join Together Boston University Public Health	http://www.jointogether.org/sa/ news/funding
National Institute of Drug Abuse Grants and Contracts	http://www.nida.nih.gov/ funding.html
National Institute of Health Grants and Contracts	http://www.nih.gov/grants
National Institute of Health Guide for Grants and Contracts	http://grants.nih/gov/grants/guide
National Resource Directory of Victim Assistance Funding	http://www.ojp.usdoj.gov/ fundopps.htm

◉ Figure 1.3. Continued

Funding Information	Location
Notre Dame Office of Research Grants Bibliography	http://www.nd.edu/~research/Pol_Proc/biblio.html
Office of Justice Programs	http://www.ojp.usdoj.gov/fundopps.htm
Office of Juvenile Justice and Delinquency Prevention	http://ojjdp.ncjrs.org/grants
Safe and Drug Free Schools U.S. Department of Education	http://www.ed.gov/offices/OESE/SDFS/grants.html
Substance Abuse Funding News	http://www.cdpublications.com/funding/saf.htm
Substance Abuse and Mental Health Service Administration	http://www.samhsa.gov/grants/grants.html
U.S. Department of Health and Human Services GrantsNet	http://www.hhs.gov/grantsnet/
U.S. Department of Health and Human Services Grant Opportunities	http://www.os.dhhs.gov/agencies/grants.html
U.S. Department of Education	http://www.ed.gov
U.S. Department of Education Budget Federal Register EDGAR (Educational Department General Administrative Regulations)	http://www.ed.gov/offices/OCFO/grants/edgar.html
U.S. Department of Education Grants and Contracts Information Office of the Chief Financial Officer	http://www.ed.gov/offices/OCFO/gcsindex.html
U.S. Government Printing Office	http://www.access.gpo.gov/su_docs/index.html

◉ Figure 1.4. Private, Corporate, and Foundation Funding

Information Source	Mail	Phone
The Directory of Corporate and Foundation Givers The Foundation Reporter The Taft Group	835 Penobscot Building, Detroit, MI 48226	800-877-8238
The Foundation Directory The Foundation Center	79 Fifth Avenue New York, NY 10003	800-424-9836

◉ Figure 1.5. Online Grantwriting Tools

Resource	Location
American Psychological Association (For APA style information)	http://www.beadsland.com/weapas/
Grant Guide Proposal Writing Short Course	http://fdncenter.org/learn/shortcourse/prop1.html
Grant Getters' Guide to the Internet	http://www.nonprofit.net/info/guide.html
U.S. Department of Education What Should I Know About ED Grants?	http://www.ed.gov/pubs/KnowAbtGrants/

CONCLUSION

Once you have found a grant program that looks as if it fits with the type of programming you want to pursue, call the contact person and have them send you an application package. There is no commitment involved in asking for this package: No one will call to check up on you or scold you for not following through. However, you need to see the application package, because it contains all the information that you will need to make the final decisions about whether or not this is the right grant program for you. Use the following checklist to make sure you have begun to take the necessary first steps toward finding sources of funding that fit with your program needs.

WHERE'S THE MONEY? *Checklist*

❑ Established access to the *Federal Register.*

❑ Identified primary sources of funding information that are accessible.

❑ Identified secondary sources of funding information that are accessible.

❑ Have identified 2–3 potential sources of funding for programming.

❑ Have ordered application packets from the sources of funding that look like they are the best match for your programming ideas.

A First Look at the Application Package 2

When you call the contact person to request an application package for their grant program, they will send you what they call a *Request for Proposals,* or RFP. The RFP, which is also an application package, will include all the necessary information and forms for you to use to apply for a particular grant. When your application package arrives, set aside some time to sit down and read through all of it. Often, the application package is a book with a stapled binding. Sometimes, it is a collection of loose papers. Keep it all together. This is everything you will need to write and submit your proposal. If you are serious about submitting a proposal under this program, do not put off doing so. Get all the necessary permissions and approvals right away so that you can get started. Do not think that you will be throwing a proposal together in a spare afternoon. That is not how grantwriting works.

COVER LETTER

Do not throw away the cover letter to your application packet. Often, this letter contains much of the necessary information you will need before beginning to organize your proposal. In this letter there will generally be mention of the due date for completed proposals, the selection criterion, reference to which issue of the federal register contains the original authorizing legislation, the total amount of funding allocated to this program, the number of grant awards they plan to make, the estimated range of awards (which tells you how much you can ask for), the project period, and a contact person for this program.

AUTHORIZING LEGISLATION

The authorizing legislation is the Congressional Act that encumbers the federal money for a grant program. A copy of the legislation will be included in the grant application package. It is generally titled as an "Act" and will read something like "The XYZ Education Act of 1998." Read this before you begin to organize and write your proposal. There will be a great deal of information in this authorizing statute that you will need to use when writing your narrative. The act will contain the information that the government found to be important, especially the causes or findings behind the creation of the legislation. These are the same findings that you will want to reflect in your statement of need. Doing so is one more way you can ensure that your project is aligned with the authorizing legislation.

Example:

Authorizing Legislation

Title IV—Safe and Drug-Free Schools and Communities Act

SEC. 4002. FINDINGS

(1) The seventh National Education Goal provides that by the year 2000, all schools in America will be free of drugs and violence and the unauthorized presence of firearms and alcohol, and offer a disciplined environment that is conducive to learning.

(2) The widespread illegal use of alcohol and other drugs among the Nation's secondary school students, and increasingly by students in elementary schools as well, constitutes a grave process. For example, data show that students who drink tend to receive lower grades and are more likely to miss school because of illness than students who do not drink.

(3) Our Nation's schools and communities are increasingly plagued by violence and crime. Approximately 3,000,000 thefts and violent crimes occur in or near our Nation's schools every year, the equivalent of more than 16,000 incidents per school day.

(4) Violence that is linked to prejudice and intolerance victimizes entire communities leading to more violence and discrimination.

(5) The tragic consequences of violence and the illegal use of alcohol and drugs by students are felt not only by students and such students' families, but by such students' communities and the Nation, which can ill afford to lose such students' skills, talents and vitality.

(6) While use of illegal drugs is a serious problem among a minority of teenagers, alcohol use is far more widespread. The proportion of high school students using alcohol, though lower than a decade ago, remains unacceptably high. By the 8th grade, 70 percent of youth report having tried alcohol and by the 12th grade,

about 88 percent have used alcohol. Alcohol use by young people can and does have adverse consequences for users, their families, communities, schools, and colleges.

(7) Alcohol and tobacco are widely used by young people. Such use can, and does, have adverse consequences for young people, their families, communities, schools, and colleges. Drug prevention programs for youth that address only controlled drugs send an erroneous message that alcohol and tobacco do not present significant problems, or that society is willing to overlook their use. To be credible, messages opposing illegal drug use by youth should address alcohol and tobacco as well.

(8) Every day approximately 3,000 children start smoking. Thirty percent of all secondary school seniors are smokers. Half of all new smokers begin smoking before the age of 14, 90 percent of such smokers begin before the age of 21, and the average age of the first use of smokeless tobacco is under the age of 10. Use of tobacco products has been linked to serious health problems. Drug education and prevention programs that include tobacco have been effective in reducing teenage use of tobacco.

(9) Drug and violence prevention programs are essential components of a comprehensive strategy to promote school safety and to reduce the demand for and use of drugs throughout the Nation. Schools and local organizations in communities throughout the Nation have a special responsibility to work together to combat the growing epidemic of violence and illegal drug use and should measure the success of their programs against clearly defined goals and objectives.

(10) Students must take greater responsibility for their own well-being, health, and safety if schools and communities are to achieve the goals of providing a safe, disciplined, and drug-free learning environment.

SEC. 4003. PURPOSE

The purpose of this title is to support programs to meet the seventh National Education Goal by preventing violence in and around schools and by strengthening programs that prevent the illegal use of alcohol, tobacco, and drugs, involve parents, and are coordinated with related Federal, State, and community efforts and resources, through the provision of Federal Assistance to—

(1) States for grants to local educational agencies and educational service agencies and consortia of such agencies to establish, operate, and improve local programs of school drug and violence prevention, early intervention, rehabilitation referral, and education

in elementary and secondary schools (including intermediate and junior high schools);

(2) States for grants to, and contract with, community-based organizations and other public and private nonprofit agencies and organizations for programs of drug and violence prevention, early intervention, rehabilitation referral, and education;

(3) States for development, training, technical assistance and coordination activities;

(4) public and private nonprofit organizations to conduct training, demonstrations, and evaluation, and to provide supplementary services for the prevention of drug use and violence among students and youth; and

(5) institutions of higher education to establish, operate, expand, and improve programs of school drug and violence prevention, education, and rehabilitation referral for students enrolled in colleges and universities.

SEC. 4004. FUNDING

There are authorized to be appropriated—

(1) $630,000,000 for fiscal year 1995, and such sums as may be necessary for each of the four succeeding fiscal years, for State grants under subpart 1; and

(2) $25,000,000 for fiscal year 1995, and such sums as may be necessary for each of the four succeeding fiscal years, for national programs under subpart 2.

Subpart 2—National Programs

SEC. 4121. FEDERAL ACTIVITIES.

(a) Program Authorized.—From funds made available to carry out this subpart under section 4004(2), the Secretary, in consultation with the Secretary of Health and Human Services, the Director of the Office of National Drug Control Policy, Chair of the Ounce of Prevention Council, and the Attorney General, shall carry out programs to prevent the illegal use of drugs and violence among, and promote safety and discipline for, students at all education levels from preschool through the post secondary level. The Secretary shall carry out such programs directly, or through grants, contracts, or cooperative agreements with public and private nonprofit organizations and individuals, or through agreements with other Federal agencies, and shall coordinate such programs with other appropriate Federal activities. Such programs may include—

(1) the development and demonstration of innovative strategies for training school personnel, parents, and members of the community, including the demonstration of model preservice training programs for prospective school personnel;

(2) demonstrations and rigorous evaluations of innovative approaches to drug and violence prevention;

(3) the provision of information on drug abuse education and prevention to the Secretary of Health and Human Services for dissemination by the clearinghouse for alcohol and drug abuse information established under section 501(d)(16) of the Public Health Service Act;

(4) the development of curricula related to child abuse prevention and education and the training of personnel to teach child abuse education and prevention to elementary and secondary school children;

(5) program evaluations in accordance with section 14701 that address issues not addressed under section 4117(a);

(6) direct services to schools and school systems afflicted with especially severe drug and violence problems;

(7) activities in communities designated as empowerment zones or enterprise communities that will connect schools to community-wide efforts to reduce drug and violence problems;

(8) developing and disseminating drug and violence prevention materials, including video-based projects and model curricula;

(9) developing and implementing a comprehensive violence prevention strategy for schools and communities, that may include conflict resolution, peer mediation, the teaching of law and legal concepts, and other activities designed to stop violence;

(10) the implementation of innovative activities, such as community service projects, designed to rebuild safe and healthy neighborhoods and increase students' sense of individual responsibility;

(11) grants to noncommercial telecommunications entities for the production and distribution of national video-based projects that provide young people with models for conflict resolution and responsible decision making;

(12) the development of educational and training programs, curricula, instructional materials, and professional training and development for preventing and reducing the incidence of crimes and conflicts motivated by hate in localities most directly affected by hate crimes; and

(13) other activities that meet unmet national needs related to the purposes of this title.

(b) Peer Review.—the Secretary shall use a peer review process in reviewing applications for funds under this section.

From this authorizing statue, we can determine that the purpose of this grant program is to explore innovative drug prevention practices and to expand programming. There do not seem to be specific restrictions on what population is served (e.g., students) or what methods or programs can be used. In fact, the language encourages innovative approaches to apply with rigorous evaluation plans so that effective new drug and violence prevention methods can be discovered. To organize this information so that it will be more usable, use Resource A, found at the back of this volume.

Example:

Meeting the Purposes of the Authorizing Statute

(Resource A)

1. What is the authorizing statute? (One sentence.)

   To establish, expand, and improve programs that will reduce rates of drug use and violence among students aged pre-K through college.

2. What is the purpose of this funding as outlined by the authorizing legislation? (E.g., increasing literacy, reducing substance abuse.) List them here.

   Strengthening programs that prevent violence in and around schools.

   Strengthening programs that prevent the use of tobacco, alcohol and other drugs.

   Strengthening programs that involve parents.

   Strengthening programs that are coordinated with community efforts and resources.

3. What is the program that you want to implement?

    Hiring additional staff at the middle school level to coordinate, improve, and expand drug and violence prevention programming.

4. How will your program further the purposes of the authorizing statute? (An application that does not further the purposes of the authorizing statute will not receive funding.)

    By hiring a designated person at the middle school (Grades 6–8), drug and violence prevention programming can be examined and expanded, parent programs can be researched and implemented, and working relationships can be established with community service providers.

Because our proposed program involves the hiring of additional staff at the middle school level to coordinate, improve, and expand drug and violence prevention programming, it will further the authorizing statute by expanding drug and violence prevention programs, parent programs, and working relationships with community service providers. This funding opportunity looks like a good fit for our program needs. If the program you want to fund does not fit with the description in the authorizing statute, then look for another source of funding.

As mentioned earlier, pay particular attention to the Causes or Findings section of the authorizing statute, because it is here that you will find the intention of the funder. In section 4002 above, for example, we learn that this grant program may favor applications like these:

> Show an interest in improving student health and academic performance through the reduction in alcohol, tobacco and other drug use (Sec. 4002[2])
>
> See the drug and violence problem as community-wide and not just school-based (Sec. 4002[4])
>
> Focus messages to youth on alcohol and tobacco as well as illegal drugs (Sec. 4002[6,7,8])
>
> Design drug and violence prevention as a part of a comprehensive strategy (Sec. 4002[9])

ELIGIBILITY

Make sure that your organization is eligible to apply for these funds. Eligibility for certain money can sometimes be very narrow and specific.

Sometimes an applicant needs to be an agency or to have nonprofit status. Determine your eligibility before writing the proposal. Information on eligibility is generally on the first few pages of the application packet.

SINGLE POINT OF CONTACT (SPOC)

If intergovernmental review is required for the grant program you are exploring, an individual will be identified as a Single Point of Contact, or SPOC. The SPOC is generally an employee of the state agency that administers programs related to the federal funding for which you are applying. If your proposal is going to be subject to a review by your state agency before being submitted to the federal government, to maximize your chances for funding, you must contact your SPOC person *before* you begin writing. The reason for this state review is so that the state can coordinate their other projects with yours or advise you on how to coordinate your project with their current initiatives and resources. Contact your SPOC first to avoid having to rewrite your proposal at the last minute.

ESTIMATED RANGE OF AWARDS

It is important to know how many awards the funding agency estimates will be made and the financial range of those awards. This information can help you determine your chances of getting an award. A grant program that has $500,000 and plans to award only five $100,000 projects will be a more difficult competition than a grant program that has $1,000,000 and plans to award one hundred $10,000 projects. If your project is a good fit with the authorizing statute and you are an eligible applicant, then you should apply for all available funds. Nevertheless, you should remember that your chances of being awarded a grant will vary depending on the amount of money and the number of awards for the grant program.

PROJECT LENGTH

Know the funding period for which awards will be made. If the award is for one year, then your plan of operation will look quite different than if the award were for a three-year project. Your application may also be rejected if you are not applying for the proper program length. Project length will be specified in the authorizing statute as well as in the cover letter.

PROHIBITED USES

Often, an application package will specify prohibited uses for the funding. Some funding programs disallow construction, consultants, computers, and other materials or equipment. Be familiar with what is not allowed and take care to not include these items in your application.

That said, there are circumstances where you may need these forbidden items in order to have an effective program and may need to include mention of them in you proposal. For example, a grant may not allow construction or remodeling expenditures, but perhaps you need to erect a few walls in order to create offices so that you will have the facilities to run your proposed program. This is fine; you simply cannot use grant money to do the construction. Use other sources of funding and include a discussion of this remodeling project in your narrative under Commitment and Capacity (see Chapter 10). If you can, show the construction costs as an in-kind contribution on your budget.

SELECTION FACTORS

Sometimes, particular factors or demographics are favored when making grant awards. This is done in an attempt to serve underserved areas or populations. Knowing if certain areas or populations are being encouraged to submit applications may work in your favor. It also may exclude you from applying for a particular grant. Understand any favored selection factors.

BACKGROUND

For most grant programs, there is a justification section in the application package, which identifies the need for this authorizing statute. Read this section carefully. Herein lie the language and the philosophy of the funder on this subject. Use these references, and use this same language in your own narrative.

SELECTION CRITERIA

The discussion of selection criteria is the most important part of the application package, because it outlines exactly which sections or narratives you need to include in your proposal. These are the criteria against which the funding agency will measure applications and use to select the best applications. You will write your proposal based on these guidelines and questions. Read through the selection criteria carefully, creating an outline to help you get organized. Each sentence in each section of the selection criteria needs to be responded to in your proposal. The sample selection criteria narrative that follows falls together into a neat outline with four sections. This outline can be used to write a proposal that will be on target with the funder's priorities, especially if you take care to use their language.

Example:

Middle School Drug Prevention and School Safety Program Coordinators

Selection Criteria

The following selection criteria will be used to evaluate applications for new grants under this competition. The maximum score for all of these criteria is 100 points.

(1) Need for the Project (25 points)
Applicants must:

(a) describe the drug, violence, or safety problems in middle schools that will be served by coordinator(s) funding by these grants;

(b) provide data on the number of students in grades five through nine who were suspended, expelled or transferred to alternative settings for drug use or violent behavior during the 12 months preceding the date of this announcement;

(c) explain how the coordinator(s) will make a difference in the drug prevention and safety problems at the middle schools to be served by this initiative; and

(d) describe how the position(s) funded by this grant will be coordinated with existing prevention programs and staff.

In determining the need for the proposed project, the following factor is considered:

(A) The extent to which specific gaps or weaknesses in services, infrastructure, or opportunities have been identified and will be addressed by the proposed project, including the nature and magnitude of those gaps or weaknesses.

(2) Quality of the Project Design (25 Points)
Applicants must:

(a) provide a detailed description of their plan for bringing about changes in the type and quality of drug prevention and school safety programs for students in grades five through nine; and

(b) describe how the community will be involved in designing and supporting these programs.

The following factors are considered in determining the quality of the project design:

(A) the extent to which the design of the proposed project is appropriate to, and will successfully address, the needs of the target population;

(B) the extent to which the proposed project is designed to build capacity and yield results that will extend beyond the period of Federal financial assistance;

(C) the extent to which the proposed project will establish linkages with other appropriate agencies and organizations providing services to the target population, including community coalitions;

(D) the extent to which the proposed project encourages parental involvement in the development and implementation of the project; and

(E) the extent to which performance feedback and continuous improvement are integral to the design of the proposed project.

(3) Adequacy of Resources (25 Points)
  Applicants must:

  (a) describe their plan for supporting and institutionalizing the coordinator(s) position into the district's permanent staffing structure, including how they will ensure its continuation when Federal funding ends;

  (b) explain how this coordinator position will be integrated into the staffing structure of the district as a whole, including where the coordinator will be housed and to whom the coordinator will report;

  (c) explain the district's plan to support the authority of the coordinator to design, select and implement prevention initiatives; and

  (d) explain how information developed by coordinators will be used by local educational agency policy makers.

Factors considered in determining the adequacy of resources are:

(A) the adequacy of support, including facilities equipment, supplies, and other resources from the applicant organization or the lead applicant organization;

(B) the extent to which the costs are reasonable in relation to the number of persons to be served and to the anticipated results and benefits;

(C) the potential for continued support of the project after Federal funding ends, including, as appropriate, the demonstrated commitment of appropriate entities to such support; and

(D) the potential for the incorporation of project purposes, activities or benefits into the ongoing program of the agency or organization at the end of Federal funding.

(4) Quality of the Project Evaluation (25 Points)
Applicants must:

(a) provide a detailed description of their plan to evaluate implementation of the coordinator initiative with particular attention to how prevention strategies have changed as a result of the coordinator's efforts and the effects on student outcomes; and

(b) agree to cooperate with any national evaluation of the coordinator(s) initiative that the Secretary may require.

In determining the quality of the project evaluation, the following factors are considered:

(A) the extent to which the methods of evaluation are appropriate to the context within which the project operates;

(B) the extent to which the methods of evaluation provide for examining the effectiveness of project implementation strategies; and

(C) the extent to which the methods of evaluation will provide performance feedback and permit the periodic assessment of progress toward achieving intended outcomes.

In this particular example, the selection criteria are divided into four sections, each worth 25 points—that is, the sections are equally weighted. In general, selection criteria are divided into four to eight sections. USDOE grants often have selection criteria sections based on the Education Department General Administrative Regulations, or EDGAR. As seen in the previous example, each section will have an assigned point value. Some selection criteria that are common but that do not appear in this example might include sustainability, the quality of key personnel, and commitment and capacity.

Knowing which sections have the greatest point value gives you an idea of where the funder's priorities are. Each section of a grant proposal will be discussed in more detail in the following chapters.

DEADLINES

The deadline for the grant program will be included in the cover letter and elsewhere in the application packet. Be aware that the deadline is often the date that your completed application is to be received, not the postmark date on your package. Can you meet the deadline with a reasonable amount of time to organize a decent proposal? Do you have a preexisting proposal that can be tweaked to meet current needs, statutes, and deadlines? Working backwards from the deadline date, build a timeline. There are many things that can take up unexpected time; unfortunately, they all come at the end of the process and can be extremely frustrating if you are not prepared for them. Before the deadline, make time for typing, printing or duplication, signatures, and packaging for mailing. Find out *now* who needs to sign the finished document. Find out everyone's vacation schedules now so there will be someone around to sign the completed Standard Form ED-424 (Application Cover Sheet) and other attachments and assurances. Depending on how many copies you will be requested to send, you may want a sturdy box for mailing: Find one now. Scrounging around in the dumpster at the eleventh hour is depressing, even though we have all done it! Plan for completion a number of days before the mailing deadline so that if a photocopier breaks down it will not jeopardize your entire proposal. A late application will be unread and unfunded.

REJECTION

A word about rejection: After all applications have been reviewed and all awards have been determined, letters of rejection are sent out on the remaining grant proposals. All grantwriters have received one or many of these. Rejection is a big part of writing grants. Rejections will happen, but they do not necessarily mean that you don't have a worthy idea. They certainly do not mean that you should give up. Applicants can request a copy of the reviewers' evaluations (but not the names of the reviewers). It is a good idea to do this. Read the comments carefully, and rewrite your proposal for resubmission with the next round.

Complete the checklist at the end of this chapter once you have found a grant program that you think will fit well with the program that you want to fund. If there are items that you are unable to check off, then you will need to back up and either look for a different source of funding or decide if there is a way to redesign your program so that it is a better fit with the authorizing statute.

A FIRST LOOK   *Checklist*

❑   Your program focus is aligned with authorizing legislation.

❑   Prohibited uses for funds do not affect your program design or implementation.

❑   Your proposal will provide services to underserved populations.

❑   The deadline for submission can be reasonably met with a decent proposal.

Write to Your Audience 3

THE READERS

While writing your proposal, remember to keep your audience in mind. In this case, your audience is not the recipients of the funding, but the grant reader. Everything you write should be done with the reader's perspective in mind. Who is the reader? A grant reader is generally a person with experience and expertise in the program area of the grant for which you are applying. They are recruited to act as consultants to read grant proposals: This is not their full-time job. They receive training in the authorizing statute for the program as well as the rules and regulations governing applications; they can work alone or in teams, depending on how the program is designed; and they read each application from cover to cover. Grant readers search the proposals for worthy projects. They read with the aid of a Technical Review Form developed specifically for this program, and on this form they list the strengths and weaknesses of your proposed project as well as the score you receive for each section (*Reviewing Applications for Discretionary Grants and Cooperative Agreements*, 1991).

Knowing that these readers review your application with the express purpose of extracting information to tally a score, your writing and organization must be very clear and specific. You want your application to be easy to read and easy to understand. You want the readers to finish reading it, set it down, and have a picture in their head of exactly what your program will be.

TECHNICAL REVIEW FORM

Readers will be rating your application against a standard checklist to measure how you have met the selection criteria of the grant program. They will use a multipage Technical Review Form, with a separate page for grading and commenting on each section. (See Figure 3.1 for an example of the cover sheet.) They will identify the strengths, weaknesses, and completeness of each section of your proposal (*Reviewing Applications for Discretionary Grants and Cooperative Agreements*, 1991).

Figure 3.1. Technical Review Form

Division of Drug-Free Schools and Communities

[name of grant program here]
(CFDA 12.345A)

APPLICANT:_____

Application #: _____

SUMMARY COMMENTS AND SCORES

Selection Criteria	Possible Points	Assigned Points
I. Concept design and contribution to improving the quality of drug and alcohol abuse education and prevention activities	30	_____
II. Relationship to drug prevention programs implemented to comply with the Drug-Free Schools and Campuses Regulations	10	_____
III. Plan of Operation	15	_____
IV. Quality of Key Personnel	10	_____
V. Evaluation Plan	20	_____
VI. Applicant's Commitment and Capacity	15	_____
Total:	100	_____

Overall Comments:

_____
_____
_____
_____
_____
_____

This Technical Review Form is created directly from the selection criteria, which is outlined in the request for proposals, generally in a narrative form. You can make your own Technical Review Form by making a careful outline of the selection criteria. The more completely your application responds to the selection criteria, the more likely you are to receive higher scores and subsequent funding.

AUTHORIZING STATUTE

Some extremely successful grantwriters recommend that you write the authorizing statute, or purpose for this grant program, on a card and keep it in front of you throughout the entire writing process (Brewer, Achilles, & Fuhriman, 1998). This is a great idea, as it will keep you focused and ensure that you are writing to the authorized statute and the readers. One of the ways in which your grant proposal will be evaluated is on its ability to connect your program ideas to the authorizing statute. You have already summarized this information on Resource A; now, clearly convey your ideas and plans and how they relate to the funder's mission in the narrative.

GETTING STARTED

Before you can consider writing a proposal, you need a strong project idea that meets the purpose of the authorizing statute. As mentioned above, by writing to meet the purpose of the authorizing statute, your chances of funding increase. It is often difficult to create a proposal for a project that completely satisfies both the needs of your school or agency and the authorizing statute. Grant programs are not always a perfect fit with your identified needs. The authorizing statute often outlines a specific program idea, population to be served, and the services and programs that will be allowed. If it meets your needs, adjust your program and do what they recommend.

READABILITY

There are a few things unrelated to content that you can do to make your grant easier to read. Sometimes these techniques will give your grant proposal enough polish to stand out from the rest. These techniques will also most certainly make the reader's job easier, and that is what you want (Knowles, 1993).

Present Yourself Well

Present yourself well; after all, you may be asking someone to give you a half a million dollars. Your grant proposal represents you and the work you do. Be neat, complete, and follow all the rules. If you submit an incomplete grant, you are saying that you are unable to pay attention to details. If you break their rules (by going over the page limit, for example, or putting things in a different order), you are communicating that you cannot follow directions or that you may break rules when it comes to spending their money.

Follow Directions

Do exactly what you are told to do and in the way you are asked to do it. If an outline is provided, use it. Follow it exactly. Use the headings that they suggest; do not make up your own. You do not want to frustrate your reader by making him or her hunt through your proposal to find information. Remember also that other applicants have followed the outline, so your grant proposal will stand out as disorganized if you do not.

Use the Forms Provided

Use all the forms they provide with the application. If the information they ask for seems redundant or irrelevant, do not assume that it is "just as good" to provide the information in a different format. Not using the forms that are provided might even disqualify your grant before anyone reads it. Use their forms, and fill in every space, even if it is with only an X or *n.a.*: You do not want your readers wondering if you unintentionally skipped a blank.

Rank Order

If you are asked to rank order items in a list, do not use Xs. They are looking for numbers showing highest priority to lowest priority. Use numbers. This might sound like a simple thing, but there are often many forms and filling them out can become confusing.

Formatting

Some grants are very specific in how they want applications formatted. Make sure you find out how they want everything to look before you start writing; doing so may save you a whole lot of time. Most grants require that you double space, that you have one-inch margins all around, that you use no smaller than a 12-point font, that you not use an italic typeface, and that you adhere to a page limit. The reasons for these strict rules are twofold. First, it standardizes the appearance of all the applications, making the judging process more objective. Second, it makes the proposal easier for the reader to read accurately. A final note on format: Do not print your final copy on an old dot-matrix printer. Documents printed on them are hard to read and do not photocopy well.

Proofread

Running a spell check on your proposal is not enough. Spell checking will often replace words with correctly spelled but incorrect words. It is important to proofread your proposal for typographical errors, misspellings, and poor grammar. Your proposal needs to be error free. Errors make a powerful statement, telling the reader that you are careless—or worse, lazy. No one is going to give a half a million dollars or a three-year contract to a careless and lazy applicant.

Style

The style of the writing should be free of jargon and too many acronyms. It is important to keep the narrative as reader-friendly as possible. To do this, use short sentences, write in an active voice, and eliminate nonessential information.

If you are not a good writer, enlist the help of someone who is. Utilize your English teachers, a parent with writing skills, or even hire a professional grantwriter. Grants have been won and lost on the clarity of the writing and the applicant's ability to describe the proposed project in a logical way.

The checklist at the end of this chapter can be used as you get organized to begin writing. It will help remind you to make an outline and follow it, to begin assigning tasks, and to follow the funder's rules for completing this application.

WRITE TO YOUR AUDIENCE   *Checklist*

❑   The Selection Criteria have been outlined before writing the narrative.

❑   The authorizing statute is written on a piece of paper and taped to your computer monitor.

❑   The forms that have been provided will be used.

❑   Formatting requirements (margin size, font, etc.) have been determined.

❑   A writer has been selected.

❑   Proofreaders have been selected.

Establishing Need 4

In order to qualify for grant money, you have to establish that you need it, really need it. You have to show that you need this grant money more than anyone else does. You do this by showing, with numbers, that there is a strong demand for the programming that you are proposing.

An application has to describe the needs that the proposed project will meet. These identified needs must be consistent with the authorizing statute that makes funding available. For example, if you are trying to receive funding for a literacy program, then describing crime rates in your community is not relevant. Describing literacy rates, staffing patterns, and the absence of resources *is* relevant.

DEMOGRAPHICS

In the beginning of this section of your proposal, you want to include brief demographic information to make your community real to the reader. Providing only one short paragraph is fine, but do not use up more space than one page. This information will set a tone for the proposal and give the reader a picture of your community. Include information about location, proximity to resources, ethnic mix, income averages, geography, and any other relevant information that will not be asked for elsewhere in the grant.

Example:

Smalltown County is a rural, agricultural county made up of 17 towns, numerous hamlets, and beautiful Trout Lake. This rural county continues to grow, with a mean income of $41K. The town of Peaceful is located in the northeast quadrant of the county at the north end of Trout Lake, an hour's drive from any major urban centers.

The town of Peaceful is the second largest in overall population in the county and has the largest population of youth ages 7–17. Of the population, 3.8% is nonwhite, 10% (190) of the 1842 families are single-parent homes, and 30% of households are married families with children. More families in Peaceful (78%) own their homes than in any other town, with an average home value of $75,000–$90,000.

All Peaceful Central School buildings are located on a single 180-acre campus. There are 684 students in the Primary School (Grades K–3), 561 students in the Intermediate School (Grades 4–6), and 929 students in the combined Junior-Senior High School (Grades 7–12). This year, we are proud to have a nationally competitive computer team, 2 students who have performed at Northeastern States Vocal Competition and Carnegie Hall, and 5 athletic teams that qualified as State Scholar-Athlete Teams with a cumulative academic average of over 90%.

To start collecting demographic data, use Resources B, C, and D in the back of this book.

ESTABLISHING NEED

Establishing need means showing, with data, why this project is necessary in your school or with this particular population. You will describe your need by using local objective data and comparing it to state or national objective data. First, you have to decide which data to collect. You do this by rereading the authorizing statute for this grant program. Is this a drug prevention grant? Then you will need data on drug use rates and current prevention resources. You will want to show that your use rates are high and your resources are low. Is this a literacy grant? Then you will want to show that your reading scores and literacy levels are low and your resources for correcting the problem are scarce. You get the idea. Use the data that shows the strongest support for your project. By establishing need, you work to convince the reader that you really have a problem that needs fixing and that the only way to do that is with these grant funds.

Objective Data

It is necessary that the data you use to describe your problem be objective. This means that rather than say things like "All kids are at risk" and "Everyone's smoking pot," you need to provide numbers. Objective data are based on measurement, not anecdote. Sources of objective data include census data, crime data, arrest data, school-based discipline data, and student survey data. There are many more places you can find accurate information.

Avoid quoting newspaper articles, news stories, opinion polls, television shows, speakers, or group discussions. Statements that begin, "Our principal says . . . , " "It is the belief of our parent group that . . . ," or "The experience of the neighboring district is . . ." are seldom followed by objective data. If you hear something compelling from any of these sources, check out the original data to see if what you heard was accurate. Chances are very good that the person reading your proposal has a firm grasp on what the current problem is in the field, or they would not have been hired to read it in the first place. If you present the problem inaccurately, the reader will notice. Make sure your data is correct and up-to-date.

Collect local data that is relevant to your project, and organize it into a chart so that it is easy to read. In Figure 4.1, a school has organized their safety and substance-abuse data into a chart. This is good baseline data, but it does not show whether there is a problem because it does not place the information in context; that is, we cannot tell if these numbers are higher or lower than local, state, or national numbers.

Comparison Data

You will notice that in Figure 4.2 there is a second set of numbers. This is called *comparison data.* Your data are meaningless without comparison data. What does it mean to say that marijuana use is at 15% in your school district? It indicates that 15% of students are smoking pot, but is that figure high or low? Better or worse than last year? If national averages are at 27%, then your rate of marijuana use is low. If state or national averages are at 9%, then your use rates are slightly elevated. If national averages are down from 34% last year, but your local marijuana use is up from 8% last year, then you are showing a trend or need.

Comparison data is also necessary when you are evaluating the effectiveness of your programming. If you are only looking at local data, and it looks like use rates are declining, that's great. But what if state and national use rates are also declining, and at a faster rate? Then your program might not be as effective as you first thought. Comparison data is critical. Your data must be presented in the big picture in order to establish a need for the program.

Target Audience

Use your data to identify the target audience for your program. Look for peaks in certain behaviors or drops in scores. Sort your data by gender, race, and grade to get a closer look at exactly which group or subgroup is most in need of program intervention. Programming should be targeted one or more years before the behavior changes are noticed in order to be effective in altering precursor behaviors or attitudes.

You can also use your data to guide your program selection and materials development. Do you find that the reading level of your target population is above or below the average? Is your target population a specific racial subgroup or socioeconomic subgroup? These details are necessary to consider when making the best decisions for programs and materials.

◉ **Figure 4.1.** School-Based Interventions

Safety and Substance Abuse

	Grade		
Incidents September 1999 to May 2000	7	8	9
Incidents of victimization*	8	9	4
Incidents of physical fighting	16	14	6
Incidents of verbal fighting**	35	35	35
Incidents of student weapon-carrying	1	1	2
Received in-school detention/suspension for ATOD (Alcohol, Tobacco, and Other Drugs) policy infractions	4	4	10
Referred for in-house substance abuse screening	4	4	9
Received in-school suspension for violent behavior (fighting, threats, harassment, pushing/shoving)	6	10	5
Received out-of-school suspension for violent behavior	9	2	3
Superintendent's hearing resulting in long-term suspension or alternative placement outside of school (for ATOD or safety-related issues only)	1	0	3
	N:186	*N:183*	*N:179*

NOTE:
* Estimated levels of victimization 3 times higher than reported numbers;
** Estimate

◉ Figure 4.2. Tobacco Use Behaviors Among 8th Graders
Smalltown School District 2000

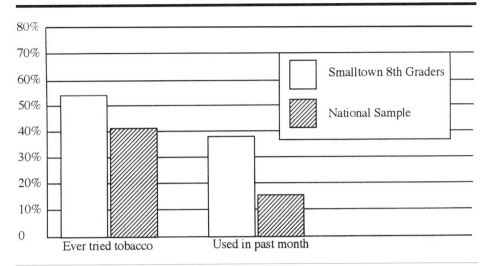

SOURCE: *American Drug and Alcohol Survey.* Administered to Smalltown School District October 1996, October 2000. *Monitoring the Future Study*, 2000. December 13, 2000. University of Michigan.

One school, for example, discovered that tobacco use peaked in the 9th–10th grades. They also found that there was not a strong tobacco prevention component in their middle school health program in Grades 7–8. A closer look at the data indicated that the tobacco use problem at the high school involved significantly more female students. They used this objective data to select an age-appropriate tobacco prevention program for their middle school, but also reviewed programs to find one that dealt specifically with young women and their smoking behaviors.

Data Presentation

A chart with comparison data and a narrative is the clearest way to present your data. Describe your interpretation of your data. What conclusions can you accurately draw? Stay objective. Be logical. Do not overdramatize the situation in your community as hopeless. Present accurate and up-to-date data, and in your narrative provide hope that your proposed program will make a difference.

Example:

Though 27% of our students are currently riding with intoxicated drivers, more than twice the national average, we are confident that Program X will reduce those numbers as it has in other schools where it has been implemented with fidelity.

Needs data will become the baseline data for the development of your evaluation plan later in this proposal. These needs data are also the foundation for writing your project objectives.

EXISTING RESOURCES

A discussion of existing resources can be a part of the needs section of your proposal or a part of the section on commitment and capacity. After looking at the needs of your population, assess which services currently exist to meet those needs and which services are missing: In short, identify the gaps. You want to show that the current services and resources are not adequate to meet the needs of your target population—and that is why you need this grant money.

When you are describing the existing resources in your community, remember to explain briefly any history your community or school has had with this type of programming. Provide information on what kinds of training or experience your staff currently has in this area. Providing training or hiring staff with more experience may become a budget issue, so the funder will want to know. What strengths separate your school from other schools that might be applying for these funds?

Collaboration is important to many funders. Do you currently work with local agencies or other service providers? Are they involved in writing this proposal? What is the collaboration history? What will their role be if you receive funding? Show that you are already working with other agencies and services to address this problem.

Finally, explain why this project should take place in your school. Why should they pick your school over the others? You may want to write a few sentences about ease of travel or unusual geographic characteristics; things that make you "average" and so make your project replicable in mainstream America; special resources, such as the financial support of a local business; or proximity to urban areas or other resources that might exist in your school or community.

The checklist at the end of this chapter reviews the same things that the reader's Technical Review Form would review. If you can answer *yes* to each of these items, then you will receive high marks from the readers as they read and score the Needs portion of your proposal. If you answer *no* to any of these items, take the time to go back and fix things before moving forward.

ESTABLISHING NEED   *Checklist*

❏   Used objective, accurate, and current data to identify needs.

❏   Identified needs are supported by the authorizing statute.

❏   Specific documentation of data is offered by the applicant as a demonstration of need.

❏   Target population for the project has been identified.

❏   Identified needs are directly related to the target population for the proposed project.

❏   Needs identified are not too many or too few for the planned time frame or project resources.

❏   Identified needs are well defined rather than generic or anecdotal.

❏   Program design and selection of materials are based on identified needs.

❏   Services that currently exist to meet needs have been identified.

❏   This site has been shown to be the best place for this program.

Goals and Objectives 5

Writing goals and objectives can be made needlessly complicated by overthinking the job. Because you know they are important, it is easy to overdo this task. Your goals and objectives are key to both your project's Plan of Operation and Evaluation Plan (see Chapters 6 and 9 for more on these plans), so they must be done well. This chapter will describe easy ways to write both goals and objectives.

GOALS

Goals are umbrella statements of the program direction. You should get your goal statement from the authorizing statute. If you are writing a literacy grant, then your goal statement will be "To increase literacy in our K–4 population." If you are applying for funding through the Safe and Drug Free Schools program, then your goal statement might be "To reduce substance use in Grades 9–12" or "To reduce vandalism on school property." Do not overwrite your goal statement; simply make it a restatement of the authorizing statute and you will be in safe waters.

OBJECTIVES

Writing objectives requires that you be a little more specific than when writing goals. An *objective* outlines a specific task to be done in order to achieve the goal of your program. An objective has only four parts, organized into a measurable statement. There are two types of objectives that you will be writing. One is called a *process objective*, which describes the implementation of your program elements. The other is called an *outcome objective*, which describes how your target population will look after receiving your program.

Process Objectives

A process objective describes how elements of your program, from program selection to training and implementation, will take place. They describe what procedure will be completed, who the person responsible for this procedure will be, how much of this service will take place (i.e., the extent of implementation), and when the deadline for completion will be.

The easiest way to create measurable process objectives that contain all the necessary elements is to create a chart. The chart should have four columns. The columns should be titled "What," "Who," "How Many/Much," and "Deadline." Use Resource E at the end of this book to help you create this chart. As you create the chart, refer back to your needs assessment data and, keeping the authorizing statute in mind, fill in the blanks. Your completed chart will look something like Figure 5.1.

These four elements are then written into single sentences. If your application requires that you itemize goals and objectives, take a close look at the following example for guidance.

Figure 5.1. Process Objectives Grid

What?	Who?	How Much/Many?	When?
Training in classroom-based violence prevention curriculum	7th–8th grade teachers	100% of them	January 2002
Use of effective prevention strategies	7th–8th grade teachers	Increase of 25%	June 2002
Training in diversity and tolerance	Noninstructional staff	75% of them	May 2002

Example:

Goal: **To reduce violence and increase tolerance, all school staff, interested parents, and community members will attend training on violence prevention, personal safety, and effective teaching techniques.**

Objectives:

1. **By January 2002, all 7th–8th grade teachers will have received training in a classroom-based violence prevention curriculum.**

2. **By June 2002, analysis of pre- and postmeasures will show use of effective prevention strategies by 7th–8th grade classroom teachers has increased by 25%.**

3. **By May 2002, 75% of district noninstructional staff will have attended training on diversity and tolerance.**

Outcome Objectives

An outcome objective describes how your target population will look after receiving your program. How will your participants be different at the end of the project? Again, the authorizing statute gives you direction on how participants are expected to be changed: They will be reading more, using fewer drugs, and engaging in fewer risk behaviors, for example. Outcome objectives describe a behavior or attitude and the target population that will be changed as a result of this program, the percentage of change that is hoped for, and when the change will be seen.

The easiest way to create measurable outcome objectives that contain these four necessary elements is again to create a chart. The chart should have four columns, titled "Behavior/Attitude," "Population," "Percentage Change," and "When." Use Resource F in the back of the book to help you create this chart. Again, refer back to your needs assessment data and, keeping the authorizing statute in mind, fill in the blanks. Your completed chart will look something like Figure 5.2.

Figure 5.2. Outcome Objectives Grid

Behavior/Attitude	Population	Percentage Change	When?
Describe district policy on tobacco use and consequences for violation	9th–10th grade students	80%	January 2002
Referrals for violating district's tobacco use policies	9th–10th grade students	Reduction of 25%	June 2002
Tobacco use	10th–11th grade students	Reduction of 15%	September 2002

These four elements are then written into a single sentence. A goal statement with outcome objectives will look like this.

Example:

Goal: **As a result of implementation of program elements, there will be an observed decrease in student smoking behaviors.**

Objectives:

1. **By January 2002, 80% of students in Grades 9–10 will be able to describe the district policy on tobacco use and consequences for violation.**

2. **By June 2002, the rate of students in Grades 9–10 who are referred for violating district tobacco use policies will be reduced by 25%.**

3. **By September 2002, students in Grades 10–11 will self-report a reduction in tobacco use of 15%.**

OBJECTIVES AND THE AUTHORIZING STATUTE

Do not lose sight of the authorizing statute as you are writing your program objectives. Does the authorizing statute say that the grant program is intended to improve literacy in underserved populations? Does it say that it is intended to reduce violence on school grounds? Does it say that it will improve community involvement with school programming? Make sure that the objectives you write all relate back to the authorizing statute, which states the purpose for the grant program.

Your objectives must also respond to the needs that you have already identified. For example, if you are writing a grant to improve literacy and you have identified an illiteracy rate of 12% in your K–4 students, then you need to write objectives that are clearly connected to that rate and population. Objectives that do not apply to that age group or that are not literacy related will not make sense to your grant reader.

Once you have written your objectives they will function as a roadmap to lead you through your project. You will be able to use these objectives to complete your Plan of Operation as well as your Evaluation Plan. So much of the rest of your proposal requires that your objectives be clear and measurable that it is a good idea to spend some time on this task.

The checklist at the end of this chapter will help focus your writing and ensure that your objectives are both measurable and based on the authorizing statute. Goals and objectives are going to be the foundation of your proposal: Do this piece well and it will shorten the amount of time it takes you to complete your application.

GOALS AND OBJECTIVES   *Checklist*

❑   Goal statements are based on the authorizing statute.

❑   Objectives are based on the authorizing statute.

❑   Objectives include both process and outcome measures.

❑   Objectives contain all four necessary elements.

❑   Objectives are measurable and realistic.

❑   There are 3–6 objectives for each goal.

Plan of Operation 6

Once you have established a need for your project and can demonstrate that it meets the authorizing statute, you must provide evidence that you have a plan for the effective implementation of your program. The *Plan of Operation* for your project is a description of exactly how you will carry out the tasks and activities you outlined in your objectives. It is the nuts and bolts of how your project will be implemented. This section of the proposal often has the highest point value, which means it is critical that you spend an appropriate amount of time creating this plan and clearly connecting your idea with the interests of the funder. This section is a high priority for the grantor, so it should be a high priority for you as well.

Preface this section with brief background information on why the project is needed or on any special circumstances of your geographic area. You have already mentioned these topics at the beginning of your proposal, but one or two refresher sentences included here will read well. Your Plan of Operation should include a timeline and a workplan. Charts work well, because they are easy to read and great for summarizing large amounts of information. This is also a place to include a brief literature review showing how your project and your selection of materials and methods fit with current theories and research.

Readers will be assessing your Plan of Operation based on the following criteria.

LITERATURE REVIEW

In order for your reader to understand why you have made the program choices that you have made, it is necessary to provide a brief (2–3 paragraphs) *literature review* to support your decisions. Review the current research on the problems that you have identified through the data review process. The research should identify programs and effective strategies. If your proposal includes outdated or disproven methods, it will be rejected.

If your activities, materials, or methods are not clearly connected to your objectives, you will need to support your decisions by referring to research that supports what you are doing. For example, suppose you are writing a proposal for a drug prevention program and you have selected to use service-focused activities. This might not make sense to the reader. How can doing volunteer work reduce substance abuse? Although the reader is an expert in the field, it is not safe to assume that she or he knows the connections between all proposed activities and outcome behaviors. Write it down and explain it.

If you do refer to research, site it APA style (American Psychological Association, 1994) and then list the complete reference on a separate sheet of paper. You can attach the list of references at the end of your proposal as one of your attachments. Keep references current if you can—no more than 5 years old. Stay away from general references like *USA Today* and *Time* magazine, and focus on scientific references.

Often, the application package will have a brief literature review included in the section on the purpose for this legislation. Read this to get started and to make sure that your program plans and selected activities are in keeping with current research on what is effective.

What follows here is a sample literature review.

Example:

Plainsville Central Schools has designed a skill-based drug-prevention program targeted at 7th–8th grade students. Current research suggests that students need to learn broader-based life skills, not just refusal skills (Sherman et al., 1997), which is why we have developed Middle School Skills for Success. Specific skills have been connected with reductions in hate crimes, intolerance, and substance abuse. Those skills include anger management, empathy, peace building, negotiation, problem solving, active listening skills, and skills for handling teasing and bullying. (Sherman et al., 1997). Our program of 25 classroom lessons includes instruction and practice time in each of these 7 skill areas. Sixty percent of program time is devoted to practice and rehearsal of these skills (Connell, Turner, & Mason, 1985). Teacher training in program content and implementation has been shown to be significant (Allison, Silverman, & Dignam, 1990). All teachers who will be using the program will attend two 8-hour days of training.

You will find the references cited in this review listed in APA style in the Reference section in the back of this book.

RESOURCES AND PERSONNEL

Project Workplan

All grants will ask you to summarize resources and personnel. A chart can be an effective way of presenting a summary of program resources and personnel. Use Resource G, which is an expansion of the worksheet for writing objectives that you used in the previous chapter, to help you create this chart. Begin by writing a single objective at the top of this sheet. In the "Tasks" column on the left, break down the objective into each of the specific tasks that will need to be done in order to fulfill the objective. You can see in Figure 6.1 that there are 12 tasks for a single objective. Some may have more, some less. Do this for each objective.

In the center column, identify the person(s) who will be responsible for each of the tasks. Finally, assign a due date for each task. The objective already lists a date, but there are many incremental things that must take place in a timely manner in order to complete each objective on schedule. By using this worksheet, you will be able to itemize the tasks that are necessary for completing each objective, to identify who is responsible for each task, and to assign a due date.

Project Timeline

Use Resource H to create a timeline. Using the workplan you have just created using Resource G, sort these tasks by date, in the order in which they must take place. The example in Figure 6.2 lists only the tasks for a single objective. Make sure that you list the tasks and dates from *all* the objectives that you have. You will notice that there is a fourth column on the Project Timeline worksheet, "Materials." In this column, list what materials will be necessary to complete each of these tasks, right down to pencils and Post-it™ notes. This list of materials will be invaluable when you develop your budget.

This completed chart now reads as a Plan of Operation. Even better, once you hire staff or turn this project over to the person in charge, there will be a very usable workplan to get them started and against which they can measure their progress. The information organized into this chart can often be submitted in this form as a formal Plan of Operation, without an accompanying narrative. If you are instructed to write a narrative, attach a Plan of Operation chart (Resource H) as an appendix to the finished proposal.

Another good reason for constructing a timeline is to show where the project milestones are and to demonstrate that they make sense in the order you have selected. Data collection first, then program selection, then implementation, then more data collection. Do the tasks and activities make sense as organized? Are you doing first things first? This completed timeline will be most important when you take your objectives and this timeline, and create an Evaluation Plan (see Chapter 9). Make sure that you are doing things in a logical and sequential order.

◉ Figure 6.1. Project Workplan

Objective: 75% of noninstructional staff will attend training in tolerance and diversity by May 2002.

Tasks	Person Responsible	Due Date
Research programs on tolerance and diversity	Project director Task force	9-30-01
Select training program	Project director Task force	9-30-01
Choose two dates for training sessions	Project director Task force	10-15-01
Contract with trainer	Project director	10-30-01
Contract with the training site	Project director	10-30-01
Create a flier advertising the training	Program assistant	12-15-01
Distribute the flier	Program assistant	12-15-01
Purchase materials	Project director Business office	2-28-02
Pretest program participants	Project director	2-28-02
Conduct training sessions	Trainers	4-12-02 5-3-02
Posttest program participants	Project director	5-31-02
Delayed posttest of program participants	Project director	11-30-02 5-24-03

Figure 6.2. Project Timeline

Date	Task	Materials	Person Responsible
9-30-01	Research programs on tolerance and diversity	Internet access university library	Project director Task force
9-30-01	Select training program		Project director Task force
10-15-01	Choose two dates for training sessions	School calendar Space availability	Project director Task force
10-30-01	Contract with trainer(s)	Phone number of trainer Selected training dates	Project director
10-30-01	Contract with the training site	Area resources Budget limits	Project director
12-15-01	Create a flier advertising the training	Computer access 6 reams of paper	Program assistant
12-15-01	Distribute flier	Postage budget	Program assistant
2-28-02	Purchase materials	Order forms Participant count	Project director Business office
2-28-02	Pretest program participants	200 pretests 200 pencils	Project director
4-12-02 5-3-02	Conduct training sessions	Rental equipment	Trainers
5-31-02	Posttest program participants	200 posttests 200 pencils	Project director
11-30-02 5-24-03	Delayed posttest of program participants	200 posttests 200 pencils	Project director

MANAGEMENT PLAN

How will you show the readers that the plan you have will be well supervised and will actually take place? The *management plan* shows that there is administration built into your grant. The project administrator will need to dedicate time to the supervision of this grant project. Have you built in the right types of supervision and administration? For example, if you are going to create counseling situations for students, then you will have to provide for some type of clinical supervision. This is a task that needs to be listed with an appropriately qualified person responsible for follow-through. If you are going to have a number of interns, then they will have to be supervised on a regular basis. Make sure that the administrative plan that you propose is doable, and that the persons put in charge have the skills and *time* to do the job you have outlined for them. You will have the opportunity to describe each person's role in more detail when you complete the Qualifications of Key Personnel portion of the proposal (see Chapter 7).

Time Schedule

The time schedule can be a problem for many proposal writers, who try to cram too much programming into the grant period. This overloading is something that the readers will be looking for. When creating the Plan of Operation, remember that it takes time to motivate people, organize training, and select and receive materials. Do you expect your teachers to attend a training the first week in September and return to have the new program/ideas fully implemented by the third week in September? That is not realistic: Change takes time. No matter how good your employees or the new materials are, change will still take time.

It will help to share your proposed timeline with those people who will be directly involved with implementing the changes or the new program. Ask them, "Can you do this?" "Am I allowing enough time for these things to take place?" "When is the best time of the year to be making changes/additions like this?" Remember also to consider holidays, school scheduling, special events, end of marking periods, and other built-in scheduling problems that may affect your proposed Plan of Operation.

For a one-year project, it is realistic to hire staff, provide training, implement new materials, and assess their effectiveness. For a three-year project, it is realistic to hire staff, provide annual or more frequent training, implement and assess new materials, and implement and measure yearly changes based on annual program evaluations.

The question to ask is not how much you *think* can be accomplished during the grant period, but how much can you, the other involved staff, and all the students *realistically expect* to accomplish during this grant period.

Activity Selection

Are your selected activities related to the authorizing statute? Readers will be looking carefully at this connection because it is the heart of the project. Will the activities you have selected move your target population closer to achieving the objectives that you have outlined?

Let us say that you have a project designed to increase student academic performance by increasing specific skills. In your proposal you have planned to take these students on four different field trips: to the zoo, the museum, the planetarium, and the aquarium. How *exactly* will participation in these field trips contribute to the skill development that is the focus of your grant? Are there specific classroom projects that will take place as a result of these outings? Are there specific skills that students will acquire as a result of these field trips? Are the field trips a way of developing skills peripheral to academics, and, if so, how will those skills strengthen their academic skills?

Describe geographic conditions of your community if they are important to understanding the activities that have been chosen. For example, readers may not understand life in rural America; so, if one of your activities is to take students to the nearest city so that they can ride elevators, escalators, and buses, you need to describe why this skill is important and why it requires a field trip.

If you cannot connect the activity that you have planned to the goals and objectives of your project, then you need to consider removing those activities. Their inclusion will weaken your proposal.

SOUND RESEARCH METHODS

Are planned activities based on sound research methods that have proven effectiveness? Have they been proven effective with *this* population? Readers will evaluate your selection of materials and methods by determining the extent to which you, the applicant, demonstrate familiarity with available training materials. Do you seem to know what you are talking about? Have you stayed current with research? A well-written literature review, as mentioned earlier in this chapter, will show the readers that you have done your reading and stayed current. You cannot fudge your way through this. Make sure that the activities and methods that you choose for inclusion in your proposed program are based on current research on effective programming.

It is also important to consider whether the program or activities that you have selected have been studied for their effectiveness with the population that you are planning to serve. If all of the research on a particular program has been done with white, middle-class students, will this program be effective with your population of mostly Hispanic students? Will the materials and concepts in the program that you have selected be appropriate for your population of nonreaders?

If you have selected a program that has been proven effective, but not with your population, you may still be able to use it. Describe in your narrative that the research on this program's effectiveness with your particular subgroup of students has been limited, but that you will be using an extensive evaluation. That way, the effectiveness of this program can be measured with your students and the results will be extremely valuable for others who are working with similar groups of students.

EQUAL ACCESS

In addition to describing how you will recruit participants and engage your target audience in your proposed program, you should describe how you will ensure that your proposed program allows equal access to *all* possible participants. Even better, explain how you will actively recruit from underserved populations. Serving underserved groups is of primary importance to most funders right now.

If you can identify who those underserved groups are and provide a plan for actively engaging and including them in your programming, you will strengthen your proposal. If you have a plan for identifying and reaching underserved or underrepresented groups, describe it. Include a description of how you will engage them, whether you will provide special services like transportation or childcare, and how you will make your facilities accessible.

General Education Provisions Act (GEPA)

When the Improving America's Schools Act (Public Law 103-382) became law in 1994, Section 427 was added to the General Education Provisions Act. This section requires applicants for federal grant awards to remove barriers from and ensure equitable access to program services.

You may be asked to write a statement describing what steps you will take to ensure equitable access to and participation in your program. What efforts will be made to remove barriers and provide services to all students, including students with special needs? The six types of barriers that are identified as impeding equitable access to programs are race, gender, national origin, color, disability, or age. Based on your own demographic data, you need to determine if these factors are issues in your community. An explanation of how you plan to address these barriers can be incorporated in different parts of your application, or can be written as a separate paragraph.

Example:

Plainsville Central School District has a policy of nondiscrimination that applies to teachers, students, and all district staff. This is an important piece of what we hope to build upon. Student focus groups have been used in the past to monitor student attitudes and opinions about changes at the school. They have included students from Alternative Education and Resource Room. We did this by running focus groups in a combined class

(Health). This practice will continue. The Substance Abuse Task Force will actively recruit members from both the Alternative Education program and the Resource Room programs. These programs serve students who have been removed from the general student population due to behavioral or learning differences. With representation from these populations on the task force, we will ensure that programming meets the needs of these students and that all student needs are considered as we implement programming. For example, if it is determined that one of the barriers to services for these students is discrimination in the community, then we will make arrangements to include community "gatekeepers" in our training and awareness sessions on tolerance and diversity. Arrangements have been made for district sign language interpreters and note takers for the visually impaired students to be included in all training and program opportunities.

DISSEMINATION AND REPLICATION

Some grants require that you describe how successful completion of your proposal will advance the field. What contribution will you be making? How will you inform your colleagues about what you have learned? Will you be presenting results at conferences? Will the program that you have developed be something that other groups serving the same population will be able implement with the same level of success? Were materials developed that can be shared with the field?

In this section of your narrative, include a discussion of any plans you have for disseminating materials and program results, both locally and on a state or national level. Discuss the replicability of your program and how broad you believe the impact might be. Be realistic, not grandiose.

CONCLUSION

In developing your Plan of Operation, you can summarize proposed resources, personnel, activity selection and implementation, and the management plan by creating a chart of goals, objectives, and tasks and creating a timeline of who will do what by what date. Add to these charts and timeline the narratives required by the funder, such as a literature review, a discussion of GEPA provisions, and information on dissemination and replicability, and you're all set.

Remember that the Plan of Operation often carries a high point value, so it is worth spending a little extra time on. Make sure it is complete. Use the following checklist to ensure that you have included all the necessary information.

PLAN OF OPERATION *Checklist*

❑ Project activities serve the purpose of the authorizing statute.

❑ Selected activities will accomplish the project objectives.

❑ Literature review provides support for program decisions.

❑ Planned activities are based on sound research and methods that have proven effectiveness.

❑ Planned activities have been proven effective with *this* population.

❑ Resources and personnel address each objective.

❑ Staffing is adequate for the proposed program.

❑ The management plan ensures effective project administration.

❑ A specific timeline for project implementation is provided.

❑ The project timeline is logical and sequential.

❑ The project workplan is in the form of a chart.

❑ The time schedule is realistic for accomplishing objectives.

❑ Access for underrepresented groups (e.g., ethnic minorities, the handicapped, or the elderly) has been established.

❑ Plans are outlined for dissemination or replication.

Quality of Key Personnel 7

In this section of your proposal, you will outline the number and quality of the staff that will be required to start, supervise, and complete your proposed project. You will need to identify titles, job descriptions, and the relevant qualifications each person will need to have. This will involve writing a brief narrative and possibly organizing a chart, if you did not already do that when you developed your management plan.

PROJECT DIRECTOR

What are the qualifications for the project director position? The role of and qualifications required for this position will be looked at closely by the readers. It is expected that this person will have the skills and experience necessary to start up and implement the proposed program. A strong project director can influence a grant decision. If you require a person to have specific degrees or certifications to hold this position, you need to justify those requirements. Why do you want to hire a person with a doctorate instead of a master's degree? Exactly what skills or experiences will that degree or certification provide, and what makes it best for your project?

Let us suppose that your school wanted to provide support groups for students who had been identified as at-risk for dropping out of school and you wanted to require that the project director be a certified social worker (CSW). Your justification may be that you anticipate students involved in the program will have multiple problems putting them at risk and that a CSW will be most capable of providing differential diagnoses and referral of students for additional services. The project director's certification would provide for an accurate diagnosis and referral, which you believe a noncertified director might not be as able to provide.

◉ Figure 7.1. Proposed Staff Distribution

Position	FT/PT	Qualifications	Salary	Responsibilities

Project Director
   Previous experience
   with program
   administration and staff
   supervision
Previous experience
   working in a school
   setting
Background in
   substance abuse
   prevention preferred
Familiarity with USDOE
   budget procedures and
   reports
	Full time	CSW	$45,000	• Supervision of staff
				• Implementation of
				  program evaluation
				• Establishment of
				  collaborative arrange-
				  ments with community
				  agencies and services
				• Attendance at task force,
				  community coalition,
				  and school administra-
				  tive staff meetings
				• Fiscal management,
				  completion of monthly
				  budget forms, quarterly
				  and annual reporting
				• Public dissemination of
				  information on program
				  events and results
				• Media contact person
				• Assessment of program
				  effectiveness

Project Coordinator
   (2 positions)
Education in counseling,
   education, or related
   field
Familiarity with
   substance abuse
   prevention
Public speaking skills
	Full time	BA/BS	$27,000	• Scheduling teacher
				  training
				• Scheduling community
				  training and awareness
				  seminars
				• Conducting training
				• Ordering and assembling
				  teacher kits
				• Keeping parent resource
				  library current
				• Writing newsletter
				• Administration of pre-
				  and posttest instruments
				• Recommending program
				  adjustments based on
				  feedback

Clerical
   Experience with
   Microsoft Word
Detail oriented
Able to work with
   deadlines
	Part time	AA/AS	$18,000
			FTE
				• Organization of large
				  mailings
				• Processing of invoices
				  and purchase orders
				• Proofreading of materials
				  and newsletter

STAFF DISTRIBUTION

Adequate Staffing

How many people will you need to adequately staff this project? You will need to determine the number of full- and part-time employees needed to complete the work you have proposed. In your proposal, include a description for each proposed position, the staffing distribution, the proposed roles and job titles, and the amount of time each person will devote to this project. Some grants will want a narrative, some will allow a chart, but it always helps to chart the information first. Use Resource I as a way of organizing this material. Remember to include in this narrative or chart a list of all of the staff to be paid from this grant, along with a description of their training and experiences, both formal and informal. Identify the level of expertise you would like to see in your staff. Will these be entry-level jobs, or will you want more experienced staff? Sometimes, practical experience, like being a mother, grandmother, or being a veteran, will be relevant to your project too. Figure 7.1 shows a completed staffing chart.

The technical reviewers—that is, the grant readers—will be assessing your staffing plan to make sure that (a) you have enough people with the right skills to do what you are proposing to do in the given timeframe, and (b) that you are not overstaffing your project.

If you have identified current school employees as the people who will staff this project, how will they have time for the additional responsibilities? Be sure to describe any changes in their job description.

Staff costs are among the largest project expenditures, so your rationale for staffing will be looked at very carefully as both a program issue and a budget issue.

Qualifications

If you will be hiring staff that has no previous experience with your program model or materials, you will probably want to provide initial staff development. The cost of initial staff development is an important budget consideration. Explore the cost of training your staff, and remember to include these expenses in your budget. If you are planning to hire staff that is already trained or experienced in your program, you can mention that in your budget narrative as a cost-saving measure.

For example, let us say that your project includes an outdoor adventure program for youths. The project requires that you hire six staff members who are already trained and experienced with this program. Your rationale, then, will indicate that providing training to inexperienced staff would take significant time and cost substantial money. By hiring pre-trained staff, you will be able to save $8,000 in training and travel costs.

Advertising

How will you recruit or advertise for these positions? Describe in just a few sentences how you will use local newspapers, regional newspapers, or professional newsletters and journals to advertise. The funder will like seeing that you are recruiting from the best sources and will be hiring the most qualified applicants. It is also important to show that you are encouraging applications from traditionally underserved populations, so describe how you will do that.

Consultants

Consultants are used in grant projects for a variety of positions now. You may be hiring someone to train your staff at the beginning of the project, to provide clinical supervision throughout the project, or to provide an evaluation component. If you will be hiring any other specialists or services, these need to be described. If possible, describe the actual consultants, the services you will be using, and why you will be using them (e.g., previous experience with them, low cost). Make sure that the use of consultants is an allowable expense within the grant program to which you are applying.

Clerical Help

Remember to include typists, secretaries, and other clerical help in your description of staffing. If you will be receiving clerical support as an in-kind service, make sure you explain this in your narrative. The grant reader might note the absence of this type of staff from your proposal and draw the conclusion that the project director will be spending valuable time with typing, mailing, and filing. Such a use of the project director's time would not be considered a good use of their grant money.

Students and Volunteers

If there are project tasks that will be done by students or volunteers, describe them. What are those tasks? How do they relate to the overall goals of your proposal? Who will supervise the volunteer activities? Is there already a volunteer group that has been involved with the writing of this proposal?

For example, say your school planned to establish a monthly student-run newsletter that reviewed all program activities. The students would collect the news, write the articles, do all the layout and duplication, and distribute the newsletter. You should outline these activities, and state that they fit with the program goals of creating student involvement and providing leadership opportunities, as well as with the dissemination of information on program progress to the community.

JOB DESCRIPTIONS

If job descriptions have been developed, especially for the project director, then attach them to your application. The information may be quicker and easier to read if it is presented in the form of a chart, as shown in Figure 7.1. A job description should include staff qualifications (i.e., level of education and experience) for this position, any necessary certifications, and a summary of responsibilities. A salary range is also included in most job descriptions, and is based on local norms, education and experience, or civil service parameters.

Personnel Policies

Hiring staff is not always quick or easy. The process of advertising, interviewing, reinterviewing, and hiring can take months. Many schools and other employers have strict policies on the handling of applications for employment; the levels or rounds of interviews and who needs to be involved that process; board review of finalists and board action on hiring, certification, and reference checks; and civil service requirements or testing. Assume that it will take three months to hire new staff. This means you need to plan program start-up activities, such as training, accordingly.

Attach Resumes

Often you will not have hired staff prior to approval of funding, so will not have resumes to attach. If, however, staff have been hired, then their resumes must be included with your application package. If the hiring of staff is still to take place, include the resume of the person who will oversee this project: Even if there is not yet a project director, there is always a boss, a clinic director, a director of community services, or a school superintendent—someone who will oversee the work of the project director.

It is now common for the grantwriter to ask the resume holder for a streamlined, shorter resume that includes only grant-relevant information for grant purposes. Not only does this save paper, but it also makes it much easier for the technical reviewers to locate necessary information. Make sure that the resumes you include highlight the qualifications necessary for the proposed project. The resumes should also reflect employee experience and a sensitivity to the target population.

To make sure you have covered all the information required to earn full points on this section of your proposal, use the following checklist to check your work. If you cannot answer *yes* to each of these questions, go back and rewrite this section of your proposal before moving on to the next section.

QUALITY OF KEY PERSONNEL   *Checklist*

❏   Key personnel are listed.

❏   Other key staff.

❏   Resumes for key personnel are attached.

❏   Job descriptions, as provided in this proposal, adequately reflect the experience and skills needed to make the proposed project work.

❏   Proposed personnel have relevant experience and qualifications. (Special attention will be paid by the reviewers to the project director.)

❏   Personnel training, if necessary, has been described and is reasonable.

❏   The amount of time each person will devote to this project is specified.

❏   Applications for employment from traditionally underserved populations are being encouraged.

❏   Existing key personnel are shown as having experience and sensitivity to the target population.

Budget Development 8

The reader of your proposal will take a close look at your budget and budget narrative. They are looking to determine if your budget is adequate and costs are reasonable. They want to see that your expenditures are consistent with the program that you proposed. Have you asked for enough money to do the project you have proposed? Have you overspent in any area? Are you spending money on the right things to get the job done? Knowing that this is how your budget will be considered, you need to take the time to create a fair and logical budget.

You will be asked as part of the application to complete both a *budget form* and a *budget narrative*. A budget form lists the amounts you are requesting and organizes them into spending categories. This is often broken down year by year. You will be asked to estimate the amounts needed for salaries, fringe benefits, overtime, substitutes, stipends, equipment, travel, supplies and materials, contracts, purchased services, and many other miscellaneous items, such as postage, phones, photocopying, and insurance.

BUDGET FORM

The Standard USDOE Budget Form ED-524, and the General Instructions for ED-524 are included in Resource M at the back of this book. You will receive both of these forms in the application package for any USDOE grant. What is included in each of these categories? Where do you get the numbers to fill in this form? Completing these forms can be overwhelming. Begin by returning to your objectives. Pour over them line by line to see what sorts of materials, supplies, equipment, and services will be required to accomplish each task. Resource H, your completed Project Timeline, itemized all the materials you anticipated using, and this will be of help to you here. You will also want a copy of Resource I, your completed Proposed Staff Distribution chart. These two resources will contain most of the information you need to complete the budget form. You will end up drafting your first budget on scrap paper. Keep these early drafts so that when it comes time to negotiate the award amount you will remember where you got various figures.

Suppose you want to train 20 teachers in a new reading program. Your costs will include the following:

Stipends for 20 teachers	$80/day × 20 =	$1600
Contract for the trainer		$1000
Training materials for 20 teachers	$6 × 20 =	$120
Classroom sets of workbooks for 400 students	$1.35 × 400 =	$540
Travel costs at 34¢ a mile for teachers to attend training		$170
Rental of space at hotel for the training	No charge	
Rental of equipment for the trainer from hotel	Overhead projector Screen	$100 $25
Lunch for 20 teachers and one trainer	$8.25 × 21 =	$173
Total cost of training		$3728

You can add these numbers up to get the cost of this training, but it is important to leave them separate so that you can plug them into the proper budget categories.

Salaries/Stipends

Your budget form will include a line for salaries and stipends. A salary may include health benefits and allowances for overtime. Stipends, or additional cash reimbursements for time and work, will also be included on this budget line.

The salary/stipend costs for your reading project, then, are

Stipends for 20 teachers	$80/day × 20 =	$1600

Note that USDOE grants distinguish salaries from training stipends. You may, therefore, want to keep these two items separate while you work out your budget.

Equipment

Equipment is defined by how much it costs. Most grant programs consider anything over $1,000 per item to be a piece of equipment. For some funders, the cutoff is lower, so check. This budget category will include more expensive items, such as computers and furniture.

Although equipment is used in the sample project described above, it was "rented" from the hotel, so this is considered a purchased service. Therefore, this sample budget would not include anything in the equipment category.

Contracts/Purchased Services

Contracts/purchased services include any service you contract for with a service provider. This includes things like hotel rooms, conference space, telephone or Internet service, repair contracts for office machines, and even roller skate rentals.

The contracts/purchased services costs for the sample project, then, are

Contract for the trainer	**$1000**

(Because the trainer is being paid to perform a specific and limited service, and is not an employee, the cost is included as a purchased service rather than a salary.)

Rental of space at hotel for the training	**No charge**

(Often, hotels will not charge for the use of their space as long as you purchase lunch for the participants.)

Rental of equipment for the trainer from hotel		
	Overhead projector	**$100**
	Screen	**$25**
Lunch for 20 teachers and one trainer	**$8.25 × 21 =**	**$173**

Supplies/Materials

No program can operate without supplies and materials. These are all the nonequipment purchases, like paper, pencils, books, videos, and computer software. Sometimes, a supply or material is a piece of office equipment that costs less than the $1,000 cutoff. Coffee pots, typewriters, furniture, and TV/VCRs may fall into this category.

In the sample budget, the supplies and materials are

Training materials for 20 teachers	**$6 × 20 =**	**$120**
Classroom sets of workbooks for 400 students	**$1.35 × 400 =**	**$540**

Travel Expenses

Travel expenses can be itemized separately for some grants, or they may be included under contracts/purchased services. Travel expenses can include the costs for all transportation, hotel rooms, registration fees, and a daily allowance for meals.

Travel expenses for the reading project include

Travel costs at 34¢ a mile for teachers to attend training	$170

This budget item is an estimate and assumes that 20 teachers will each drive approximately 25 miles roundtrip to attend the training.

One must examine each objective in the proposal to determine what it will cost, where the costs will come from, and which budget categories those costs fall into. Break each task down into the actual costs that will be required to complete them. In some cases you will have to make estimates. In some cases you will have to make phone calls to determine the costs of consultants or program materials. Do not include items that are not mentioned in your narrative or objectives.

Fringe Benefits

Fringe benefits include FICA (Federal Insurance Contributions Act), health insurance, Medicare, any additional medical plans like dental, vision or prescription riders, and any other benefits that may have been negotiated by the staff. Figuring these costs is not as hard as it may seem. Contact the school business office or the financial officer for your agency, and ask for help. Generally, your organization will have a formula for working this out, and these people can do it with you over the phone.

Total Direct Costs

The total direct cost of your project is the sum of all the items—items number 1–8 on the Budget Form ED-524. Simply add them up and write down the total.

Indirect Costs

Most schools and businesses have a cost of doing business. This is called the *indirect cost*, or how much it will cost the school to maintain buildings, process the grant-related papers, and to perform other business office functions. A grant will use the services of many people who are not directly funded by the grant. The indirect cost is how schools receive compensation for this type of unseen labor. Most schools have a small percentage that they multiply by the direct cost. Check with your business office or financial officer.

Total Costs

The total cost for a project is the sum of the total direct costs, indirect costs, and training stipends. This is the bottom line, literally.

You will want to give yourself a half-day to organize all of these numbers. Always use the budget forms that have been provided with the application. *Do not use your own or substitute forms from another grant or project.* Your readers will be comparing your budget to those of other applicants who followed directions and used the right forms. You want your proposal to stand out, but not because you did not follow simple directions.

BUDGET NARRATIVE

The budget narrative is where you describe your planned expenditures and justify anything that might be unusual. This means that you have the chance to explain how the hourly rates for instructors were determined, offer an itemization of fringe benefits, demonstrating why participant stipends are necessary, and more. For example, your equipment costs might be high for the first year. In your narrative, you can explain that these are start-up expenses. Travel expenses might be high. In your narrative you can explain that your area is remote and travel costs are generally higher for that reason.

Remember to also explain why some budget categories might be lower than average. For example, if you are implementing a classroom program, but your budget shows no purchased materials for students, you might want to explain that you have a fraternal organization that will be purchasing all of those materials (and provide the cost of those materials) for your school. If you have generous in-kind contributions like this, remember to attach a letter from that contributing organization at the end of your grant confirming the in-kind gift.

Use the budget narrative as an opportunity to explain anything unusual in the budget. The budget narrative can be written as straight text, which would read as a description of the numbers on the budget form, as if you were explaining the budget to a room full of people. If you use a straight narrative, be careful not to start describing programming: Stick to the budget. Alternatively, you can write the narrative section by section or provide it footnote style, responding only to specific areas of the budget.

Example:

Budget Narrative—Initial Year

Personnel: **The salary for the project director is competitive at $35K. This is lower than national salaries for similar positions, but the cost of living in this community is low. This salary, which is about the same as a salary for a teacher with 10 years of experience, will ensure that we are able to hire a** staff member with a background in substance abuse and violence prevention and who has had experience working within a school system. The training specialist is currently a half-time employee of the school district. The district will pay $12K to increase her hours to full-time so that she can dedicate 20 hours/week on this project.

Fringe benefits: The fringe benefits amount includes FICA ($2292), health insurance ($4054), Medicare ($536), and a Med. 105 Plan ($150). It is in keeping with current contract negotiations.

Travel: Travel includes funding for one round-trip flight to Washington, DC ($500), as required by the grant, 7 room nights ($700), reimbursement for meals ($200), and $400 for reimbursement of mileage (1176 miles ($0.34) for attendance at other meetings and training opportunities throughout the year. Ours is a rural district, so travel expenses by car to events will be slightly elevated.

Equipment: It is not anticipated that any equipment will need to be purchased. The school district will allow use of all projection equipment, photocopiers, and computers for this program.

Supplies: During the initial year, we will make a one-time purchase of skill-based violence prevention curriculum materials for all 7th–8th grade teachers. Assuming $200/curriculum ($\times$ 20 teachers), that comes to $4000. We will also need to purchase one desk ($450), chair ($60), telephone ($120), and various secretarial supplies ($300).

Contractual: A large part of our initial year will involve the training of staff, faculty, students, parents, and community members. This $1000 will be applied to trainers' fees.

Construction: No construction.

Other: None

Total Direct Costs: $51,762

Total Indirect Costs: $776

Training Stipends: $2,000 at $100/day ($\times$ 20 teachers) is budgeted for summer teacher training stipends. These costs are in keeping with current contract negotiations.

Total Costs: $52,538

Adequacy of Budget

Is the budget adequate to carry out all proposed project activities? Your reader will be reviewing your budget carefully. One thing that will be considered is whether you have budgeted enough money to carry out all of the proposed activities that you outlined in your program plan. Did you miss anything? They will want to see, both in your budget and in the narrative, that you have planned for all details and will not run short of funds. You need to budget enough money to be able to complete the program that you say you will complete.

Reasonability

The "reasonableness" of project costs will also be considered by your readers. That means the readers will take a close look to see if you are overspending or if there is a way to do your program at a reduced cost. Is it necessary to hold your training at the most expensive hotel in town? Is it necessary to purchase expensive dinners for everyone at every training event? Do you really need 30 new computers, or will 15 accomplish the same goals? You need to review your own budget with these questions of reasonability in mind.

Administrative Costs

How much of the project's total cost is devoted to administrative expenses? Is your budget heavy with administration? One thing that readers will be looking for is a budget that is written to maintain employees who are not actually dedicated to this project. People try to do this all the time as a way of avoiding layoffs. Avoid writing a budget that has high administrative costs if you can. Overspending in this area will become obvious when your budget is read next to other budgets that are not doing this.

It is also important to keep administrative costs as low as possible. Does your project require a full-time administrator as well as a full-time project director? Take a close look at the employee distribution. If you only have one or two employees involved with implementing this project, then full-time administration might not be necessary. Administrative positions and costs are expensive and can often overwhelm a budget. High administrative costs will result in less money for programming, and funders want their money spent on program implementation. Be reasonable.

Justification

Are all budget items sufficiently justified? Remember to explain the larger or more unusual budget items in your narrative. If you need these items to accomplish your program goals, then a few sentences of explanation will be fine.

Padding

Padding is a way of getting additional money that can then be used for nonprogram expenses. This has been done since the beginning of time— or at least since the beginning of grantwriting. Your reader has been instructed to look for padding in your budget and to consider that when scoring your proposal. It is one thing to slightly overestimate your budget needs so that you will not run out of money. This is considered acceptable practice. However, adding hundreds or thousands of dollars where you will not need it for this particular project is unethical. If you pad your budget, it will be noticed and you will be asked to explain it. Avoid this.

YEARS TWO AND THREE

Consecutive years in a multiyear budget should reflect cost-of-living salary increases as well as decreases in equipment and training expenses. The latter are often considered start-up expenses, so should be concentrated in the first year.

NEGOTIATIONS

If your proposal is being considered for funding, you will receive a call from the funding agency to negotiate your budget. You will be asked questions about where your budget could be cut down, where you might be able to find in-kind contributions, or where your school district or organization might be able to find funds to cover some of the expenses. This is the funder's way of making sure that they can fund more applications by not overspending. Because you might get this call, you need to be sure that you can justify every penny that you have requested. This is where the saved draft budgets sheets will come in handy, reminding you of all the spending details. If cuts to your budget will result in reductions to your program plan, explain that in your negotiations. If there are program cuts you are willing to make, offer them.

Using the checklist at the end of this chapter, review your current budget plan. Make sure that you can answer *yes* to each item. If not, revise your budget until you can. Your budget may be the most closely scrutinized portion of your proposal, so take great care in doing a thorough and honest job.

BUDGET DEVELOPMENT *Checklist*

- ❏ Used provided budget forms.
- ❏ Budget is adequate to carry out all proposed activities.
- ❏ Project costs are reasonable.
- ❏ Budget includes
  - ❏ salaries for all personnel
  - ❏ fringe benefits for employees
  - ❏ travel
  - ❏ equipment
  - ❏ supplies/materials
  - ❏ contracts/purchased services (e.g., training)
  - ❏ construction (when allowed)
  - ❏ indirect cost amount
  - ❏ stipends
- ❏ All objectives have been broken down by tasks and costs.
- ❏ All items in the budget are also mentioned in the application narrative and objectives.
- ❏ All unusual or large budget items are explained in the narrative.
- ❏ Administrative costs are kept low.
- ❏ Budget narrative reflects in-kind contributions.
- ❏ There is no padding.
- ❏ Budget shows decreases in equipment and training costs over the project period.

Evaluation Plan 9

The evaluation plan is the section of most proposals where people lose points. I know of one grant reader who reads this section first, and if its weak or absent he simply sets the grant aside as unfundable. Evaluation is intimidating, but very important to getting your proposal funded. This chapter will simplify the process.

Evaluation will determine how well your project achieved its objectives. Your evaluation plan will therefore need to demonstrate two things: first, that you did everything that you said you were going to do and, second, that you reduced the need you identified at the start of your proposal. The former is an *evaluation of program implementation,* the latter a *measure of program impact.*

The evaluation plan needs to be built into the project from the beginning. Even before the project period begins, the grantwriter has begun the process of evaluation by collecting baseline data to use in writing the proposal. This baseline data and objectives you have already written are the backbone of your evaluation plan.

An evaluation plan for the purpose of a winning a USDOE or similar grant does not have to be a piece of airtight scientific research. It does, however, have to be thoughtful and logical. You will not have to perform any higher-order statistical manipulations with the numbers, but you will have to do basic math and percentages. You can do this.

A good evaluation of program implementation and program impact will cost money. Some federal grants will even require that you hire an outside evaluator. Remember to build these costs into your budget. Include the cost of materials, the time it will take for someone to synthesize the results, and the consulting fees if you hire evaluators. Your budget should reflect expenditures related to evaluation costs.

IMPLEMENTATION EVALUATION

The results of an implementation evaluation show whether or not you did what you said you were going to do. Did you offer the number of training sessions that you specified? Did you involve the number of participants that you said you would? Did you get all the teachers trained that you had planned for? Did you train everyone by the deadline specified? Did trained teachers implement the new materials?

Timeline

Collect the process objectives specific to program implementation that you wrote (Chapter 5, Resource E). List these process objectives on a separate piece of paper in order by the date by which they are to be accomplished. This is easiest if you have completed the Process Objective worksheet (Resource E). To evaluate process objectives, you merely need to indicate whether or not they were done. By creating a timeline for program implementation from your process objectives, you have started an evaluation plan for program implementation.

Below is an example of the start of a timeline for program implementation. Five process objectives are listed. For each objective, a data collection plan has been developed.

Example:

Timeline for Training Program Implementation

1. **By December 2001, 75% of school staff will attend training on classroom-based violence prevention curriculum.**

    September 2001, a list of school staff attending curriculum training on violence prevention will be established.

    September 2001, administration of teacher pretest on classroom conflict resolution techniques.

    December 2001, based on attendance at violence prevention training, it will be determined if 75% of staff has been trained.

    December 2001, three separate training dates will have been offered to teachers for curriculum training on violence prevention.

    June 2002, administration of teacher posttest on classroom conflict resolution techniques.

2. **By May 2002, 60% of noninstructional staff will attend training on violence prevention.**

    September 2001, a list of noninstructional staff attending training on violence prevention will be established.

    May 2002, based on attendance at violence prevention training, it will be determined if 75% of noninstructional staff has been trained.

    May 2002, three separate training dates on violence prevention will have been offered to noninstructional staff.

3. By June 2002, the Substance Abuse Task Force will have met a minimum of four times.

   October 2001, student representatives will be appointed to the Substance Abuse Task Force.

   October 2001, Alternative Education and Resource Room representatives (students) will be appointed to the Substance Abuse Task Force.

   June 2002, Substance Abuse Task Force will have meet four times by this date.

4. By December 2001, 100% of 7th–8th grade students will have attended awareness events on diversity and tolerance.

   December 2001, three awareness events on diversity and tolerance will have been made available to 7th–8th grade students.

   September 2001, a list of 7th–8th grade students attending training on diversity and tolerance will be established.

   December 2001, based on attendance at training on diversity and tolerance, it will be determined if 100% of students have been trained.

5. By June 2002, there will be attendance of at least 20 parents at various staff development opportunities.

   September 2001, arrangements will be made for collecting the names of parents who attend districtwide training events.

   May 2002, there will be 20 or more names on the list of parents who have attended districtwide training events.

For each objective, the proposal writer determined which data collection methods would most accurately measure completion or success. Those data collection tasks were then listed by date (see Figure 9.1). This timeline becomes an excellent management tool for data collection. You can monitor exactly where you are with program implementation and data collection based on where you are on this timeline.

Classroom Implementation

After receiving training, how completely and accurately are your staff or teachers implementing the new program? Implementation fidelity is an important piece of your evaluation. It is not enough to simply train your teachers; you must design a system for monitoring the degree of classroom implementation of the new program and the fidelity with which it is implemented. This can be done with the use of classroom observers, teacher feedback sheets, or occasional classroom monitoring visits. In the previous example, it was done with the use of a pre- and posttests for teachers on how often they use the conflict resolution skills in their class-

Figure 9.1. Data Collection Timeline

Due Date	Task	X
September 2001	Administration of teacher pretest on classroom conflict resolution techniques.	_____
September 2001	A list of school staff attending curriculum training on violence prevention will be established.	_____
September 2001	A list of noninstructional staff attending training on violence prevention will be established.	_____
September 2001	A list of 7th–8th grade students attending training on diversity and tolerance will be established.	_____
September 2001	Arrangements will be made for collecting the names of parents who attend districtwide training events.	_____
October 2001	Student representatives will be appointed to the Substance Abuse Task Force.	_____
October 2001	Alternative Education and Resource Room representatives (students) will be appointed to the Substance Abuse Task Force.	_____
December 2001	Three separate training dates will have been offered to teachers for curriculum training on violence prevention.	_____
December 2001	Based on attendance at violence prevention training, it will be determined if 75% of staff has been trained.	_____
December 2001	Three awareness events on diversity and tolerance will have been made available to 7th–8th grade students.	_____
December 2001	Based on attendance at training on diversity and tolerance, it will be determined if 100% of students have been trained.	_____
May 2002	Three separate training dates on violence prevention will have been offered to noninstructional staff.	_____
May 2002	Based on attendance at violence prevention training, it will be determined if 75% of noninstructional staff has been trained.	_____
May 2002	There will be 20 or more names on the list of parents who have attended districtwide training events.	_____
June 2002	Administration of teacher posttest on classroom conflict resolution techniques.	_____
June 2002	The Substance Abuse Task Force will have met four times by this date.	_____

rooms. It is important that you include a plan for monitoring the accuracy and completeness of program implementation in your evaluation plan.

Participant Feedback

You will also want to build into your evaluation plan a feedback system for program participants. It is important to gather experiential information from them as they participate in the program. This can be done by administering participant feedback forms during and after program participation. You can use this information to adjust programming so that it is more comfortable for the next group of participants.

Example:

Participant Feedback

| 1. Did you enjoy this program? | 1 | 2 | 3 | 4 | 5 |

| 2. Did you learn anything while participating in this program? | 1 | 2 | 3 | 4 | 5 |

| 3. Is after school the most convenient time of day for this type of program? | 1 | 2 | 3 | 4 | 5 |

4. What could be added to this program?

5. What could be taken out of this program?

OUTCOME EVALUATION

Evaluating the impact of your program is a little more complicated than evaluating implementation. Impact, or outcome, evaluation requires more planning. You need to have an evaluation plan in place before the program begins. This portion of your evaluation will determine whether or not you reduced the need you identified at the start of this proposal. Ideally, you will be showing that Program X caused behavior change Y.

If you have completed the Outcome Objective worksheet (Resource F), then you already have an idea of what changes you would like to see in program participant behaviors. These changes in participants need to be kept consistent with the authorizing statute of the grant. If the authorizing statute says that this money is intended to improve literacy, then showing that you have improved the self-esteem of your participants is not an effective outcome measure—unless you can find research that shows that increases in self-esteem are directly correlated with increases in reading skills. Your evaluation plan needs to show that you have increased literacy, or have changed participant attitudes/behaviors in the direction that you proposed in your original objectives. This is the measure that lets you know if your program has been successful.

Baseline Data

The first step in creating an outcome evaluation plan is to collect baseline data. You will want current, preprogram measures of the behavior or attitude that you are trying to change. If you are trying to reduce criminal behaviors, then you will need current measures of criminal behaviors for your target population. Collect this data from school discipline records, probation department data, and arrest records. If you are trying to improve math and reading skills, then you will want current math and reading achievement scores for your target population. If you are trying to reduce substance abuse, then you will want current measures of substance use rates for your target population.

You can then compile this baseline data into a chart and include it as an attachment to your grant (see Figure 4.1). This indicates to the readers that you have a grasp of basic program evaluation, and that by collecting preprogram rates and frequencies of the targeted behavior you have already taken the first step toward measuring the effectiveness of your program.

Evaluation Design

An outcome evaluation plan is a glorified schedule for data collection. Your evaluation design should be able to show four things:

1. Participant behavior changed in the desired direction as a result of participating in your program.

2. Your program was more effective than no program.

3. Your program was more effective than another program.

4. Your program was effective with a broad population of participants and in a range of settings (which indicates the program's potential for replication).

So, how will you know if your program has been successful in these four areas? It's all in the data collection.

One Group Pretest/Posttest Design

In a *one group pretest/posttest design* evaluation, you begin with a review of the baseline data, which lets you know where your target population is with regards to the behavior you are trying to change. (You already did this when you established a need for the program.) The next step in this evaluation design is to conduct the program. After participation in the program, you then re-collect data to see if it is different from original baseline measures. For example, preprogram rates of vandalism might have been 12 incidents per month. The same vandalism measures after the program might be only 6 incidents per month. Below is a simple diagram of this evaluation design:

Data collection—Program—Data collection

This evaluation process is easy to do, but will not yield the most accurate data on your program's effectiveness.

Control Group Design

How can you tell that changes in vandalism rates were caused by your program rather than the change in seasons, a change in police activity, a change in reporting, or a concurrent program? You can't. To determine whether it was your program that caused the change, you need to use a *control group design.* A control group is a sample the same size and with the same characteristics as those who will receive your program, only they do not participate in the actual program. Here is a diagram of this evaluation design:

Data collection—Program—Data collection
Data collection—No Program—Data collection

There are some easy ways to create a control group. You can split your original sample and randomly provide your program to half of it. Or, you can select a classroom in your school or similar grade in a neighboring school as your control. By comparing the second round of data collection between the group that got your program and the control group, you will be able to say with more authority that your program caused changes in participant behaviors.

Comparison Group Design

If you want to take the comparative method of the control group design a step further, you can add a third group that receives a different program than yours:

Data collection—Program A—Data Collection
Data collection—Program B—Data collection
Data collection—No program—Data collection

With the comparison group design, final data collection between the three groups allows you to determine whether or not the programs were more effective than no program at all, and which of the two programs were best at changing participant behavior.

The two programs do not have to be different programs. They can be the same program with different delivery styles, conditions, or student participants. You can vary the length of the program, the frequency of the program, the facilitators, the participants, the materials, anything you want, as long as you measure beforehand and then again after the program is completed.

Collecting Data

Reliability and Validity

It is important that the sources and tools you use to collect data be both reliable and accurate. *Reliability* means consistency; it means that the tool you use to collect data will be predictable in its results. If you develop a questionnaire for students about their smoking behaviors and the results are variable—sometimes way above or below state or national norms—there is no consistency to the results. This means you probably have an unreliable instrument and data from this instrument is unreliable. This means you need to find a different data source.

Validity is more about accuracy. Does the questionnaire on smoking behavior actually measure the student's smoking behavior? It is possible that the way the questions are worded or the way the survey is administered (with an adult watching perhaps) may encourage students to "fake good" or lie. What you learn may be what students want you to believe, not what their actual smoking behavior is. The questionnaire may actually measure the amount of trust students feel, not the amount they smoke.

In order to ensure that the data you have are both reliable and valid, it is good practice to collect data from two or more places.

Pretests

Pretests are used to collect data on participant behaviors and attitudes before programs begin. Collect data specific to the change you would like to see in your participants. If you anticipate that your program will reduce smoking behavior, then you need an accurate preprogram measure of smoking rates for participants.

En Route Tests

En route tests are used to collect participant feedback about the content and feel of the program for process evaluation. Changes in program content, length, location, or leaders are made based on this information.

Posttests

Immediately following a program, participants take a posttest to measure changes in the targeted behavior. If the pretest measured smoking rates, then the posttest needs to measure smoking rates. In many cases, the pre- and posttest are the same instrument. Pretest and posttest data can be compared to determine the direction and magnitude of change in participant behaviors.

Delayed Posttests

To determine the enduring impact of your program, you will have to collect data 6 months after participants have completed the program, and then again at one year postprogram. By collecting data for an extended period of time after the program is over, you can measure the endurance or decay of program effects. Delayed posttests are the true measure of program effectiveness.

The Proposal

There are no specific forms to fill out for the evaluation plan portion of your proposal. The readers are expecting to see a narrative, or perhaps a data collection chart similar to Figure 9.1. In some cases, the evaluation portion of the proposal is where you list your goals and objectives. Creating a chart will make your evaluation plan clear to your readers and will work as a management tool later as you are implementing your program. An evaluation narrative should accompany this chart.

Example:

A teacher survey will be administered during the first week of September 2001 to all 7th–8th grade teachers. This survey will be readministered in June 2002 to all 7th–8th grade teachers. Results will indicate that classroom teachers are using more effective conflict resolution strategies as a result of program changes and teacher training throughout the school year.

It is expected that student behavioral incidents related to violence or substance abuse, as measured by current data collection (student use surveys, school referrals, and behavioral incident reports), will *increase* during the first year of this initiative as staff and students improve in their ability to identify and refer students and as building administrators improve in their record keeping. This initial increase will be seen as a success in the project director's efforts to streamline data collection efforts and ensure that resources and services will be made more accessible to all students.

Data on contacts and referrals with local agencies and services will be maintained to determine if there is an increase in student access and use of off-campus services.

Attendance at all training and awareness sessions will be taken to determine the percentage of students, teachers, staff, parents, and community members who are participating.

MODEL PROGRAMS

The readers will be looking for an evaluation design able to prove that your proposed project has benefited participants in the direction and magnitude that you predict. They will also keep an eye out for projects that have a likelihood for replication with other populations or in other areas. Will your evaluation design provide information on the applicability of this program to the general population? Will the funding agency be able to learn about the effectiveness of your proposed methods and materials? If your evaluation design is strong, it will provide this information.

Use the checklist at the end of this chapter after you have drafted your evaluation plan. If there are items that you cannot answer *yes* to, revise your evaluation plan.

EVALUATION PLAN   *Checklist*

❑   Project objectives are measurable.

❑   The evaluation plan is detailed, including method and frequency of data collection, and measuring both process and outcome.

❑   Objective baseline data is already collected and has been used to determine the needs of the target population.

❑   Ongoing data collection methods are described, including a timeline for data collection, selection of evaluation instruments, who is responsible, and what data will be collected.

❑   The evaluation plan will produce valid and reliable data.

❑   A timeline for implementation of program elements has been developed.

❑   A plan for monitoring the accuracy and completeness of program implementation is included.

❑   Subjective participant feedback is used to make minor mid-course adjustments.

❑   The evaluation methods are appropriate to the proposed project.

❑   An evaluation design is included (e.g., one group pretest/posttest, control group design, or comparison group design).

❑   The evaluation will determine the effectiveness of the project activities in meeting the project objectives.

❑   Evaluation results provide information on the potential for this project to be replicated.

❑   If necessary, an outside evaluator is named in the application.

❑   Budget reflects expenditures related to evaluation costs.

Commitment and Capacity 10

ADEQUACY OF RESOURCES

In the Adequacy of Resources section of your proposal, you must show that you have the means necessary to carry out this project. Basic resources include facilities, equipment, supplies, personnel expertise/ experience, and any cooperative agreements with area groups or organizations. What you want the reader to understand is that, if funded, you are more than able to implement the project that you have proposed.

This section is generally short but needs to contain details. List the resources, both equipment and personnel. Describe the networking, will it be formal or informal? Are there shared services? Is there a local business interested in supporting your project? Will you have interns?

Facilities

Are the facilities you plan to use adequate to the program that you plan to implement? Will you have enough space of the right kind and in the right place? If you are proposing a youth drop-in center, then your facilities need to be where youth have access by foot, not a suite of offices in a remote area of the city. If you are proposing a midnight basketball component, do you have access to a basketball court during those hours? Do you have an arrangement with the owners of that court? Can you show this working relationship with a letter of support or by describing previous cooperative agreements with these owners?

When describing the physical space you will be using, remember to mention whether facilities are accessible to all potential participants. If they are not currently accessible, what are your plans for making needed adjustments?

If you have space and facilities secured at the time that you are writing your proposal, include a letter of agreement indicating that this relationship and space arrangement exists.

Equipment and Supplies

Do you have the equipment you will need for your proposed project? List the resources that you have available to you. Include computers, equipment, space, supplies, and access to services. If there are things missing, describe how you plan to get them. Will you be using grant monies, receiving donations, or developing cooperative arrangements?

Example:

The project director will be provided with dedicated office space in the Counseling Suite in the Junior-Senior High School. A desk and chair, file cabinets, office supplies, a private phone line, and mailbox in the main office will be established before employment begins. Also available in the Counseling Suite are private meeting rooms, and a large group room equipped with chairs and a chalkboard. There will be full access to the school-based copy center, computer center, Internet and e-mail, and secretarial support. The project director will have access to additional training as necessary in new programs and techniques, and time off for travel to Washington, D.C., for grant-related training.

Interagency Coordination

You have targeted the population to be served by your program. Now you need to enlist the involvement of any service providers in your area that also serve that population. By doing this, you ensure that you are, first and foremost, not duplicating preexisting services and programs. Although you think your program idea is brilliant, someone else might have had the same idea 10 years ago and established an agency or program that is already providing the same services. You may not know this unless you start networking. However, your reader will most likely know if your proposed program is duplicating services that already exist. Remember that your reader is an expert in the field of this grant program.

You will also want to find services or personnel that can help with your proposed projects. There may be programs and services that fit well with what you are planning to do and that want to be involved with your project. You may also find sources of expertise, interns, or volunteers. Enlist the participation of any agencies with similar missions. Remember to get a letter of support from these agencies to include with your application as an attachment.

Experience and Expertise

As already noted in Chapter 7, you will want to establish that the personnel who will be implementing your proposed project have the experience and expertise necessary to do an exceptional job. Describe their experience with this type of programming and their professional skills as administrators or directors. Mention the amount of time that they will be dedicating to this project. Highlight previous successes.

If you will be hiring a small staff, how will you ensure that you get the best applicants? Are you hiring enough staff to get the job done? What other sources of experience and expertise will you have access to? Is there a university nearby? Do you have any cooperative arrangements with different staff or departments there? Is there a local business or agency with notable expertise in this area? Do you have a cooperative relationship with them?

You may also want to list any existing committees or groups that have demonstrated previous successes in the area of your program. Remember to include any recognition and awards that these groups have received.

Lastly, how committed are you to this project? How committed are school administrators or other leaders? What sacrifices or changes will be made to adopt these new program ideas? How many people are involved with the planning? Is there enthusiasm for what might be coming, and how can you document that? (E.g., through attendance at planning meetings or volunteerism).

SUSTAINABILITY

The portion of the application devoted to sustainability, often tucked into Adequacy of Resources, asks you to explain how you intend to continue this project once this particular grant program runs out. Once all the equipment is purchased and training has taken place you may only need to fund salaries. How will you do this? Who will be responsible? Will another agency or business be involved? Will costs be shared? What has happened in the past with the continuation of programs after grant funds were gone?

The reader will be looking for the long-term viability of your project, your ability to sustain this program once the grant money is gone. Talk about past success with securing funds. You can argue that the success of this particular project will make you attractive to other funders. Some programs dedicate time throughout the project to seek out additional grant money. Some districts have access to grantwriting services as well. Be specific about current and projected funding streams.

It is okay to say that, after reviewing the results of the program, your district or agency will decide if the program's impact justifies the use of district funds for continuation. You can also say that this project is finite, with a start and an end. It is possible that, once you have purchased materials, trained teachers, and ensured implementation of the new programs, program staff will not be required beyond the grant period.

Use the checklist at the end of this chapter to make sure that you have included all possible evidence of commitment, adequacy of resources, and sustainability in this portion of your narrative.

COMMITMENT AND CAPACITY   *Checklist*

❏ Proposed facilities are large enough for proposed programming.

❏ Facilities are well located for program activities.

❏ Facilities for all aspects of project are accessible to all participants.

❏ Letters of agreement or contracts are in place for facility rental, if necessary.

❏ Equipment available is adequate for program activities.

❏ Evidence of interagency coordination is presented.

❏ Proposed staff are adequate to get the job done.

❏ Proposed staff have the necessary experience and expertise.

❏ Proposed program has access to off-site sources of expertise.

❏ Cooperative agreements exist with key agencies.

❏ There is a plan for continued funding.

Cover Sheets, Abstracts, and Other Miscellany 11

A sample of forms, and instructions for completing them, are included in Resource M at the end of this book. Please refer to the appropriate form for each section of this chapter.

COVER SHEET

All applications for federal assistance use the same cover sheet. This is the standard form ED-424. The application package that you initially received contains this standard cover sheet form and line-by-line instructions for completing it. Follow these instructions carefully and fill in every space. Do not leave the reviewer guessing about whether you overlooked something.

Data Universal Numbering System (DUNS) Number

The DUNS Number is required on item 2 of the cover sheet ED-424. This is a unique nine-digit number that conveys no identifying information about your school or agency. This is a way of objectively cataloging and tracking proposals. Chances are good that your school already has an assigned DUNS number. You can find out by calling 1-800-333-0505. If your school or agency does not have one, then you can get one assigned at no charge. The DUNS number request form can be found at http://www.dnb.com/. Then click on the button labeled "D&B D.U.N.S number."

PROTECTION OF HUMAN SUBJECTS IN RESEARCH

Item 12 on ED-424 asks if your project will involve any research with human subjects. There is a discussion of this in the Instructions for ED-424 form, and further information on the Attachment to ED-424. Copies of both are included in Resource M. The primary source for information on the rules governing the protection of human subjects in research is found in Title 34 of the CFR, part 97 Subpart A (basic policy), Subpart D (additional protections for children). You can read these rules on the USDOE Website at http://www.ed.gov/offices/OCFO/humansub.htm.

The question is, is your proposal considered research on human subjects? In most cases, educational projects that take place at the K–12 level are exempt from these regulations. Projects that take place at the college level may be required to be reviewed by their Institutional Review Board. Read the Instructions for ED-424 and Attachment to ED-424 carefully to make sure that you are in compliance.

TABLE OF CONTENTS

Figure 11.1. Sample Table of Contents

(Pay close attention to the order in which your grant program wants to have things organized.)

Proposal Section	*Page*
Cover Sheet	1
Table of Contents	2
Abstract	3
Narrative	4
Meeting the Purposes of the Authorizing Statute	4
Project Objectives	5
Extent of Need for the Project	6
Plan of Operation	10
Quality of Key Personnel	17
Budget	19
Evaluation Plan	21
Adequacy of Resources	24
Appendices [There may be a page limit]	
Assurances/Certifications	26
Letters of Cooperation	33
Resumes	37
Job Descriptions	39
References	42

Most grant proposals require that you include a table of contents. This will be the last page that you write. Pay close attention to the order in which the grant program to which you are applying wants you to organize your application. Do things exactly the way they ask you to, even if you do not think it makes sense. Your proposal should have each page numbered in order before you create your table of contents. See Figure 11.1 for a sample Table of Contents.

ABSTRACT

The abstract is a brief summary of your identified needs, project objectives, plan of operation, and the intended outcomes of your program. This will be the first page of narrative and the first thing that your reader reads. Try to make it an engaging, hopeful snapshot of your proposed program.

Often, there are length restrictions to the abstract—one page or ten lines, for example—or you will be provided with an Abstract Form to complete instead. Follow the rules. If the funding agency provides a form, use it. If they suggest a length restriction, stick to it. If no restrictions on length are given, do not exceed one paragraph. This should be the second to last piece of the proposal that you write (the table of contents being the last). If you save this for the end, writing it will be much easier. Use Resource J, Writing an Abstract, to help you: Fill in the blanks on this worksheet, then smooth it out into a narrative.

Example:

Abstract

By hiring a School Safety Specialist under this grant program, Plainsville Central School hopes to reduce student behaviors of violence in Grades 7–12. We will do this by (1) revising and updating district policies related to violence; (2) providing training to school staff, interested parents, and community members on violence prevention and personal safety; (3) enhancing our working relationships with community services; (4) expanding our mental health referral services into the Junior High School; (5) promoting student involvement in planning all aspects of these programs; and (6) increasing parent involvement with district activities. We will measure our success with these objectives over the three-year grant period by using preexisting planning groups, providing the very best quality training and materials, involving students in all levels of program development, and carefully monitoring our risk indicators by continual collection and review of objective data. It is our hope that, with hard work and adherence to the project timeline, we will be able to reduce student behaviors of violence by 10%–15% by the year 2004.

ATTACHMENTS

Appendices and Assurances

Attachments to your proposal will include those that are supplemental to your narrative, such as references and evaluation instruments, and those that will be required, such as resumes of key personnel, letters of agreement, and assurances. The latter are standard forms that will be provided by the grantor. Please refer to Resource M at the end of this book for examples. It is required that these forms be signed and dated by the superintendent, CEO, director, or other ultimate supervisor of programs and funding for your school or organization. Sometimes, ink color for these signatures is specified. Follow directions.

These standard forms may include the following:

1. **ED-424**—Standard Cover Page for applications for federal education assistance.

2. **ED-524**—Budget Form for nonconstruction programs.

3. **ED-524, Section B**—This additional budget form will be used if the grant program requires that you show matching funds or other nonfederal resources.

4. **Standard Form 424B**—Assurances for nonconstruction programs. This form, assuring compliance with the specified regulations, needs to be signed by the superintendent/CEO/director of your school or organization.

5. **ED 80-0013**—Certifications Regarding Lobbying (Debarment, Suspension and Other Responsibility Matters, and Drug Free Workplace Requirements). This form will also need to be signed by the superintendent/CEO/director of your school or organization.

6. **ED 80-0014**—Certification Regarding Debarment, Suspension, Ineligibility and Voluntary Exclusion (Lower Tier Covered Transactions). This assures that your school or agency is in good legal standing entering into this financial agreement.

7. **Standard Form LLL**—Disclosure of Lobbying Activities.

8. **Attachment to ED-424**—Protection of Human Subjects in Research. To be used only if nonexempt research activities involving human subjects are planned at any time during the proposed project period.

Resumes of Key Personnel

Often, key personnel involved in the project develop a short one-page resume specifically for use with grant proposals. See Chapter 7 for more on this.

Letters of Support

You will need to include letters of support from the agencies and organizations that will be involved with the proposed project. Try to include letters of support from organizations that have made generous in-kind financial contributions to your project. These should be current, on letterhead, and with original signatures. Do not attach letters of support that are on thermal fax paper or from a past project. It often helps if you send the supporting agency a draft of the type of letter you will need from them. Give them ample time to write and send you a decent letter through the post. Contact them at the beginning of the proposal-writing process if you can.

Support letters should include the following:

- A description of the relationship you have with this agency

- The role of the cooperating agency in this proposed project (e.g., acting as trainer or evaluator)

- Commitment of time, money, services, space, or equipment that will benefit your proposed project

Proposals with strong cooperative arrangements will be favored, because these relationships increase the chances for program success.

References

If possible, justify your choices of program, activities, and methods by citing supportive research. In the brief literature review portion of your proposal, you only needed to refer to the results of the research, then note the last name of the researcher and the date of the research in parentheses, such as *(Knowles, 2001)*. This is the APA (American Psychological Association) style of notation. Attach a list of complete references, including any and all research that you have cited in your narrative, at the end of your proposal. A research-based proposal has a better chance of being funded. Look at the page of references in the back of this book for an example of proper formatting.

SUBMITTING YOUR APPLICATION

Order

Take care to organize your final application, making sure that it includes all the necessary pieces and that they are in the proper order. Generally, an application is organized as follows (though there can be differences depending on the grant program, so check):

1. Cover page (Standard Form ED-424 for USDOE applications)

2. Table of contents (requires that every page be numbered)

3. Project abstract

4. Program narrative, often limited in length. Adhere strictly to these guidelines.

5. Budget (Standard Form ED-524 for USDOE applications)

   Budget narrative and justification

6. Assurances (Standard Form ED-424B for USDOE applications)

   Certification Regarding Lobbying

   Certification Regarding Debarment

   Standard Form—LLL

   Signatures in the proper color of ink

Copies

You will be asked to submit from 2–5 complete photocopies of your application. Make sure that all copies are clean, complete, readable, and dark enough. Mail them all together as one package.

Mailing

Most federal grant programs require that the CFDA number and alpha suffix of the competition under which you are applying be written on the outside of the mailing envelope or box. Do not forget to do this.

In most cases, once you have mailed your application package, you will receive a Grant Applications Receipt of Acknowledgment. If you do not receive one after 2–3 weeks, you need to call the Application Control Center or similar receiving office to make sure they have received your application. Sending the package by Certified Receipt will also let you know that it has been received.

AFTER SUBMISSION

Stay Prepared

Once you have done the initial research, organization, and writing to complete a proposal, you can use it, or pieces of it, for additional funding opportunities. Keep your proposal on disk, and as additional opportunities for funding come along adjust the narrative portions to meet the selection criteria of the new program. Most grant programs ask for the same types of information. Once you have written one good proposal, you can resubmit it in a number of places. Of course, you must always update the numbers and data.

Keep Current Data

Now that you know what data you need to collect and where it is, establish a system of data collection so that you can keep these numbers current. Though some data will only be available annually (like survey data), you will find it is much easier to compile other data on a month-to-month basis. Often, doing it this way will show interesting trends, such as months with higher vandalism or truancy rates. Unless the data are broken down by months, that trend will not be visible. Do not throw old data away: Trends are as important as current data.

Rewriting

It is okay if you do not win your first few grants. Grantwriting is a skill that you can learn if you have a little persistence. The first thing to do with a rejected proposal is to get reviewer comments and to read through them carefully. Make any changes and improvements *now*, while the process is still fresh in your head. Not all the reviewer changes will be possible or necessary, but most will be. These comments indicate the reasons you lost points. Once you have the proposal rewritten, you are ready to resubmit next year.

Use the checklist at the end of this chapter to review all the final details of organizing and submitting your proposal.

COVER SHEETS, ABSTRACTS, AND OTHER MISCELLANY

Checklist

❑ Read all instructions carefully, because they often contain small details, like "Indicate original in red ink."

❑ Remember to get proof of your mailing date (use registered mail).

❑ Double check to make sure you are sending the application to the right address.

❑ Send the right number of copies.

❑ Address the package correctly. Some require the grant program to be identified on an outside corner of the envelope or box.

❑ Make sure your packet is arranged in the suggested order.

❑ Include support letters, resumes, and references.

❑ Establish systems for continued collection of data.

❑ Get reviewer comments and make time to rewrite the proposal immediately.

Resource A

Meeting the Purposes
of the Authorizing Statute

Every program is authorized by legislation or a statute. Grants are awarded to projects that best reflect the purposes of the statute. Be aware of the authorizing statute's purpose and make sure that it is reflected in your application.

1. What is the authorizing statute? (One sentence)

   _____

   _____

2. What are the objectives of this project as outlined by the authorizing legislation? (E.g., increasing literacy, reducing substance abuse). List them here.

   _____

   _____

   _____

   _____

3. What is the program that you want to implement?

   _____

   _____

4. How will your program further the purposes of the authorizing statute? (An application that does not further the purposes of the authorizing statute will not receive funding.)

   _____

   _____

Resource B

Community and School Demographics

Keeping the following information current will greatly simplify the writing of your next proposal.

Community Demographics

1. Urban, rural, or mixed

2. Descriptive demographics on the location of the school district relative to cities, urban areas, and resources

3. Number of school buildings and grade levels of each (include private schools)

4. Population of cities, towns, and villages served by the district

5. Major businesses

6. Per capita income

7. Unemployment/ employment trends

Student/School Demographics

1. Absenteeism

2. Retention rate (failures), drop outs

3. Standard test scores (math, reading, English)

4. Percentage SPED (special education), vocational, and alternative

5. Number of teachers and professional staff

6. Ratio of teachers to students by grade level

7. Level of staff training

8. Average years of experience of staff

9. Staff turnover rate

10. Percentage of minority professional staff

11. Percentage of students home schooled

12. Percentage of students home tutored

13. Salary rates

14. Per pupil expenditure for programs

Resource C

Student Enrollment Data Collection Form

	AA*	AI	AS	HS	WH	Other	Total M/F	Total Enrollment
Pre-K								
K								
1								
2								
3								
4								
5								
6								
7								
8								
9								
10								
11								
12								
Nontraditional								
Alternative								
Adult Ed GED								

*AA	African American	HS	Hispanic
AI	American Indian	WH	Caucasian
AS	Asian	Other	Others not specified

Resource D

Summary Teacher Education/Expertise

	BA	MA	MA + 45	Specialist	PhD/Ed	Other	Total
Pre-K							
K							
1							
2							
3							
4							
5							
6							
7							
8							
9							
10							
11							
12							
Alternative							
Adult							

Resource E

Process Objectives

What?	Who?	How Much/Many?	When?

Resource F

Outcome Objectives

Behavior/Attitude	Population	% Change	When?

Resource G

Project Workplan

Objective:		
Tasks	**Person Responsible**	**Due Date**

Resource H

Project Timeline

Date	Task	Materials	Person Responsible

Resource I

Proposed Staff Distribution

POSITION	FT/PT	QUALS	SALARY	RESPONSIBILITIES

Resource J

Writing an Abstract

Project title: _____
_____

Name of your
school/agency: _____
_____

Project description: _____
_____
_____
_____

Target population: _____

Goal statement: _____
_____
_____

Objectives: 1. _____
_____
2. _____
_____
3. _____
_____
4. _____
_____

Duration of program: _____

Evaluation design: 1. _____
_____
2. _____
_____
3. _____
_____

Resource K

Glossary

Applicant: The person, school, agency, or group that is applying for funds.

Application: A written request for funding. *See* Proposal.

Authorizing Statute: The mission or purpose of the funder described in a congressional act. Outlines specifications for program development.

Award: The amount of money that is granted to an applicant.

Budget: An estimate of how much money will be needed anywhere spending is anticipated.

Call for Proposals: The published announcement that funding is available for a specific type of programming. *See* RFP.

EDGAR: Educational Department General Administrative Regulations. A standard selection criteria for Education Department (ED) grants.

Enabling Legislation: Specifies the population to be served and the services and programs that will be allowed.

Equipment: Most grant programs have a cost cutoff that separates equipment from supplies. Anything over $500 or $1000 (it can vary) is considered equipment. Anything below that amount is considered a supply.

Facilities: The physical location where the programming will be taking place. This includes space and equipment.

501(c)(3): The section of the tax code that defines nonprofit or tax-exempt organizations.

GEPA: General Education Provisions Act, Section 427. This requires that applicants for discretionary grant programs include information on how they will ensure equitable access to proposed programming.

Grant Proposal: The completed grant application. A written request for funding that includes an outline of needs, project plan, personnel, budget, and evaluation plan. It is called a proposal before it has been approved for funding.

Grants Officer: A person from the Grants and Contracts Services (GCS) who interprets grant management policies to the grant reviewers/readers. Grants officers answer questions, advise reviewers on process, and explain the key provisions of EDGAR. They do not provide input into the actual review of applications. A grants officer is a resource person for the readers.

In-Kind Contributions: A contribution of supplies, services, equipment, or space. Different from a monetary contribution.

Literature Review: A reading and summary of all current research on effective methods, materials and techniques in the area for which you will be writing your grant. Current literature and research should be no more than 5–7 years old and published in peer-reviewed journals.

Peer Review: A process where your proposal will be read by reviewers considered to be your peers in the field. Peer reviewers are selected because they have experience and expertise in the area of the grant.

Program Officer: A member of the program office staff, the office that has publicized the availability of the grant funds and written the regulations concerning them. Program officers facilitate the review process. They will check all technical review forms for completeness and accuracy, and will prepare a summary recommendation for each application.

Project: The product or service that you plan to offer if you receive the funding.

Proposal: A completed application for funding.

Reviewer: The grant reader. Selected based on general and specialized experience and expertise in the program area. These readers review the applications based on rigid selection criteria. They are the primary source of objective assessment and accurate scoring of applications.

RFA: Request for Applications. See RFP.

RFP: Request for Proposal. A funder issues an RFP when it wants applicants to submit proposals for funding.

Selection Criteria: The evaluation standards used to assess the strengths and weaknesses of an application.

SPOC: Single Point of Contact. The person at a state agency who will review and comment on your proposal before it is submitted. This review is sometimes required to ensure that your programming fits with the state's mission.

Technical Review Form: This form is used by the readers of the completed applications to "grade" the applications.

Resource L

Grantwriting FAQs

Where can I find out about available grant money?

The best source of information on educational grant monies or federal grants is the USDOE Website, http://www.ed.gov. Current and future grant programs will be listed there along with contact information. The *Federal Register* will publish USDOE application notices, which will provide you with basic program and contact information. There are many primary, secondary, and online sources of funding information listed in Chapter 1 of this book to get you started.

What is a CFDA number?

All federal discretionary grants are assigned an identification number based on the *Catalog of Federal Domestic Assistance (CFDA)*.

How do I get an application package?

The easiest way is to visit the USDOE Website, http://www.ed.gov. Have the name or *CFDA* number of the grant program you are interested in when you log on. *Federal Register* notices of grant competitions will include a phone number and a name of someone who can send you the application package.

How do I know if I am eligible to apply for a particular grant?

If you have access to the *CFR*, you can look up the particular grant program by its *CFDA* number to review eligibility requirements. Or, you can call the contact person and request an application package, which will also list eligibility requirements.

What is meant by "funding priorities"?

Funding priorities are activities that will be the focus of funding for a particular year or funding period. If a funding priority is focused on programs conducted after school hours, then your proposal should be focused on that type of program, too.

What is the "authorizing statute"?

The authorizing statute is the Congressional Act that describes the purpose of the funding.

What if I don't write so good?

Enlist the help of someone who writes well and who will be able to transfer your ideas into proposal format. The readability and accuracy of your grant is important in helping the reader picture the program you are proposing.

How much do I ask for?

The application package will contain information on how much money has been set aside for this program, how many awards they anticipate making, and will even recommend a range or ceiling for you. Stay within these recommendations.

How long will writing a grant take?

Writing your first grant takes the longest. If you work fast, you can probably throw something together in a week. Three weeks is better. Assume it will take you half a day to assemble and synthesize preexisting data in order to establish need. Doing a literature review for research that supports your program ideas will take a day. It will take you another half day to write the goals and objectives if you itemize them and sort them in different ways to make program implementation timelines and use them to start drafting costs for materials and training. Designing your first budget will require sitting down with someone from your business office and having them walk you through the mechanics of figuring fringe benefits and indirect cost. This could take an hour.

Remember that there will be a number of people and service providers involved with implementing this grant if you do win it, so you will want them involved ahead of time, having them help you to shape various program elements. This will require a meeting or two to brainstorm roles and responsibilities. After those meetings, it will take another few hours to write the narratives for your Plan of Operation, Quality of Key Personnel, and Commitment and Capacity sections.

Attachments and assurances, collecting signatures, and writing the abstract, an introduction, and a table of contents will all take more time than you anticipate. So will copying and getting everything ready to be mailed.

If I design a thorough evaluation plan, am I still exempt from Protection of Human Subjects in Research regulations?

In most cases, programs that are implemented in an educational setting are exempt from these regulations. However, this depends on exactly what it is you are planning to do. Check the USDOE Website, http://www.ed.gov/offices/OCFO/humansub/pitfalls.html, which explains this in more detail.

What is an indirect cost rate?

A percentage of the direct cost items. Most schools have an established indirect cost rate. Check with your business office or financial officer.

What if I miss the deadline?

The USDOE and most other funders will not accept applications that arrive after the published deadline.

Does a high score guarantee that I will be funded?

No, unfortunately, it does not. A high score puts you in the game, but does not guarantee funding. Funders may run out of money because there were many exemplary applications. They may also need to fulfill geographic distribution requirements, assigning awards to specific areas of the country. This could work for you or against you.

Who actually reviews my application?

A grant reviewer, or reader, will be recruited by the funder to do so. Readers have expertise in the subject area of the grant program and may receive extra training by the funder prior to reviewing proposals.

How do they keep the review process fair?

There is a strict selection criteria and point system developed for each grant program. Reviewers rate each grant against this criteria by using a Technical Review Form. Reviewers often work in teams.

What are the most common grantwriting mistakes?

Failure to develop a solid evaluation plan, which is often the result of writing immeasurable objectives, and not connecting the project to the authorizing statute.

How will I know if I have won a grant?

Generally, there will be a phone call where an award offer is made or negotiated. Sometimes, you simply receive an official Grant Award Notification (GAN) letter. You will also receive a written notice if you have *not* been selected for funding.

Will I always get the amount I have asked for?

Sometimes, but not always. Occasionally the reviewers will suggest changes to your proposed program that will result in a budget decrease. If a proposed budget seems inflated, you will be offered less. It also happens that the funder may not have the funds that were anticipated, so will have to give fewer or smaller awards.

How long will it take to actually get money?

After the grant deadline, there is generally a few months' wait before award letters go out. Award letters will be mailed before the start of the project period. You will not receive any money with your award letter. After receiving the award letter, you need to establish necessary grant accounts with the USDOE or other funder, then you submit a request for payment. Funds are transferred electronically, anywhere from 1 to 3 days after submitting a payment request.

Resource M

FORMS

Application for Federal Education Assistance

Note: If available, please provide application package on diskette and specify the file format.

U.S. Department of Education
Form Approved
OMB No. 1875-0106
Exp. 09/30/2001

Applicant Information

1. Name and Address

   Legal Name:_____

   Address: _____

   Organizational Unit _____

   _____

   City _____ State ____ County ____ ZIP Code + 4 ____-____

2. Applicant's D-U-N-S Number [ ][ ][ ][ ][ ][ ][ ][ ]

3. Applicant's T-I-N [ ][ ]-[ ][ ][ ][ ][ ][ ]

4. Catalog of Federal Domestic Assistance #: **8 4** [ ][ ][ ] ☞

5. Project Director:_____

   Address:_____

   _____ _____ _____
   City   State   ZIP Code + 4

   Tel. #: ( )_____-_____ Fax #: ( )_____-_____

   E-Mail Address:_____

6. Is the applicant delinquent on any Federal debt? ☐ Yes ☐ No
   (If "Yes," attach an explanation.)

   Title:_____
   _____

7. Type of Applicant *(Enter appropriate letter in the box.)* [ ]

A State	H Independent School District
B County	I Public College or University
C Municipal	J Private, Non-Profit College or University
D Township	K Indian Tribe
E Interstate	L Individual
E Intermunicipal	M Private, Non-Profit College or University
G Special District	N Other (Specify):_____

8. Novice Applicant ☐ Yes ☐ No

Application Information

9. Type of Submission:

   —PreApplication
   ☐ Construction
   ☐ Non-Construction

   —Application
   ☐ Construction
   ☐ Non-Construction

10. Is application subject to review by Executive Order 12372 process?

    ☐ Yes *(Date made available to the Executive Order 12372 process for review):* ____/____/_____

    ☐ No *(If "No," check appropriate box below.)*
    ☐ Program is not covered by E.O. 12372.
    ☐ Program has not been selected by State for review.

11. Proposed Project Dates:

Start Date:	End Date:
____/____/_____	____/____/_____

12. Are any research activities involving human subjects planned at any time during the proposed project period? ☐ Yes ☐ No

    a. If "Yes," Exemption(s) #:

    b. Assurance of Compliance #:

    OR

    c. IRB approval date: _____
    ☐ Full IRB **or**
    ☐ Expedited Review

13. Descriptive Title of Applicant's Project:

Estimated Funding

14a. Federal	$	.00
b. Applicant	$	.00
c. State	$	.00
d. Local	$	.00
e. Other	$	.00
f. Program Income	$	.00
g. TOTAL	$	.00

Authorized Representative Information

15. To the best of my knowledge and belief, all data in this preapplication/application are true and correct. The document has been duly authorized by the governing body of the applicant and the applicant will comply with the attached assurances if the assistance is awarded.

    a. Typed Name of Authorized Representative

    b. Title

    c. Tel. #: ( )_____-_____ Fax #: ( )_____-_____

    d. E-Mail Address:

    e. Signature of Authorized Representative   Date:____/____/____

1. **Legal Name and Address.** Enter the legal name of applicant and the name of the primary organizational unit which will undertake the assistance activity.

2. **D-U-N-S Number.** Enter the applicant's D-U-N-S Number. If your organization does not have a D-U-N-S Number, you can obtain the number by calling 1-800-333-0505 or by completing a D-U-N-S Number Request Form. The form can be obtained via the Internet at the following URL: http://www.dnb.com.

3. **Employer Identification Number.** Enter the employer's identification number as assigned by the Internal Revenue Service.

4. **Catalog of Federal Domestic Assistance (CFDA) Number.** Enter the CFDA number and title of the program under which assistance is requested.

5. **Project Director.** Name, address, telephone and fax numbers, and e-mail address of the person to be contacted on matters involving this application.

6. **Federal Debt Delinquency.** Check "Yes" if the applicant's organization is delinquent on any Federal debt. (This question refers to the applicant's organization and not to the person who signs as the authorized representative. Categories of debt include delinquent audit disallowances, loans and taxes.) Otherwise, check "No."

7. **Type of Applicant.** Enter the appropriate letter in the box provided.

8. **Novice Applicant.** Check "Yes" only if assistance is being requested under a program that gives special consideration to novice applicants and you meet the program requirements for novice applicants. By checking "Yes" the applicant certifies that it meets the novice applicant requirements specified by ED. Otherwise, check "No."

9. **Type of Submission.** Self-explanatory.

10. **Executive Order 12372.** Check "Yes" if the application is subject to review by Executive Order 12372. Also, please enter the month, date, and four (4) digit year (e.g., 12/12/2000). Applicants should contact the State Single Point of Contact (SPOC) for Federal Executive Order 12372 to determine whether the application is subject to the State intergovernmental review process. Otherwise, check "No."

11. **Proposed Project Dates.** Please enter the month, date, and four (4) digit year (e.g., 12/12/2000).

12. **Human Subjects.** Check "Yes" <u>or</u> "No". If research activities involving human subjects are <u>not</u> planned <u>at any time</u> during the proposed project period, check "No." **The remaining parts of item 12 are then not applicable.**

If research activities involving human subjects, whether or not exempt from Federal regulations for the protection of human subjects, <u>are</u> planned <u>at any time</u> during the proposed project period, either at the applicant organization or at any other performance site or collaborating institution, check "Yes." If <u>all</u> the research activities are designated to be exempt under the regulations, enter, in item 12a, the exemption number(s) corresponding to one or more of the six exemption categories listed in "Protection of Human Subjects in Research" attached to this form. Provide sufficient information in the application to allow a determination that the designated exemptions in item 12a, are appropriate. **Provide this narrative information in an "Item 12/Protection of Human Subjects Attachment" and insert this attachment immediately following the ED 424 face page. Skip the remaining parts of item 12.**

If <u>some or all</u> of the planned research activities involving human subjects are covered (nonexempt), skip item 12a and continue with the remaining parts of item 12, as noted below. In addition, follow the instructions in "Protection of Human Subjects in Research" attached to this form to prepare the six-point narrative about the nonexempt activities. **Provide this six-point narrative in an "Item 12/**

Protection of Human Subjects Attachment" and insert this attachment immediately following the ED 424 face page.

If the applicant organization has an approved **Multiple Project Assurance of Compliance** on file with the Grants Policy and Oversight Staff (GPOS), U.S. Department of Education, or with the Office for Protection from Research Risks (OPRR), National Institutes of Health, U.S. Department of Health and Human Services, that covers the specific activity, enter the Assurance number in item 12b and the date of approval by the Institutional Review Board (IRB) of the proposed activities in item 12c. This date must be no earlier than one year before the receipt date for which the application is submitted and must include the four (4) digit year (e.g., 2000). Check the type of IRB review in the appropriate box. An IRB may use the expedited review procedure if it complies with the requirements of 34 CFR 97.110. If the IRB review is delayed beyond the submission of the application, enter "Pending" in item 12c. If your application is recommended/selected for funding, a follow-up certification of IRB approval from an official signing for the applicant organization must be sent to and received by the designated ED official within 30 days after a specific formal request from the designated ED official. **If the applicant organization does not have** on file with GPOS or OPRR **an approved Assurance of Compliance** that covers the proposed research activity, enter "None" in item 12b and skip 12c. In this case, the applicant organization, by the signature on the application, is declaring that it will comply with 34 CFR 97 within 30 days after a specific formal request from the designated ED official for the Assurance(s) and IRB certifications.

13. **Project Title.** Enter a brief descriptive title of the project. If more than one program is involved, you should append an explanation on a separate sheet. If appropriate (e.g., construction or real property projects), attach a map showing project location. For preapplications, use a separate sheet to provide a summary description of this project.

14. **Estimated Funding.** Amount requested or to be contributed during the first funding/budget period by each contributor. Value of in-kind contributions should be included on appropriate lines as applicable. If the action will result in a dollar change to an existing award, indicate <u>only</u> the amount of the change. For decreases, enclose the amounts in parentheses. If both basic and supplemental amounts are included, show breakdown on an attached sheet. For multiple program funding, use totals and show breakdown using same categories as item 14.

15. **Certification.** To be signed by the authorized representative of the applicant. A copy of the governing body's authorization for you to sign this application as official representative must be on file in the applicant's office.

Be sure to enter the telephone and fax number and e-mail address of the authorized representative. Also, in item 15e, please enter the month, date, and four (4) digit year (e.g., 12/12/2000) in the date signed field.

Paperwork Burden Statement

According to the Paperwork Reduction Act of 1995, no persons are required to respond to a collection of information unless such collection displays a valid OMB control number. The valid OMB control number for this information collection is **1875-0106**. The time required to complete this information collection is estimated to average between 15 and 45 minutes per response, including the time to review instructions, search existing data resources, gather the data needed, and complete and review the information collection. **If you have any comments concerning the accuracy of the estimate(s) or suggestions for improving this form, please write to:** U.S. Department of Education, Washington, D.C. 20202-4651. **If you have comments or concerns regarding the status of your individual submission of this form write directly to:** Joyce I. Mays, Application Control Center, U.S. Department of Education, 7th and D Streets, S.W. ROB-3, Room 3633, Washington, D.C. 20202-4725.

PROTECTION OF HUMAN SUBJECTS IN RESEARCH
(Attachment to ED 424)

I. Instructions to Applicants about the Narrative Information that Must be Provided if Research Activities Involving Human Subjects are Planned

If you marked item 12 on the application "Yes" and designated exemptions in 12a , **(all research activities are exempt),** provide sufficient information in the application to allow a determination that the designated exemptions are appropriate. Research involving human subjects that is exempt from the regulations is discussed under **II.B. "Exemptions,"** below. The Narrative must be succinct. **Provide this information in an "Item 12/Protection of Human Subjects Attachment" and insert this attachment immediately following the ED 424 face page.**

If you marked "Yes" to item 12 on the face page, and designated no exemptions from the regulations **(some or all of the research activities are nonexempt),** address the following six points for each nonexempt activity. In addition, if research involving human subjects will take place at collaborating site(s) or other performance site(s), provide this information before discussing the six points. Although no specific page limitation applies to this section of the application, be succinct. Provide the six-point narrative and discussion of other performance sites in an **"Item 12/Protection of Human Subjects Attachment" and insert this attachment immediately following the ED 424 face page.**

(1) Provide a detailed description of the proposed involvement of human subjects. Describe the characteristics of the subject population, including their anticipated number, age range, and health status. Identify the criteria for inclusion or exclusion of any subpopulation. Explain the rationale for the involvement of special classes of subjects, such as children, children with disabilities, adults with disabilities, persons with mental disabilities, pregnant women, prisoners, institutionalized individuals, or others who are likely to be vulnerable.

(2) Identify the sources of research material obtained. from individually identifiable living human subjects in the form of specimens, records, or data. Indicate whether the material or data will be obtained specifically for research purposes or whether use will be made of existing specimens, records, or data.

(3) Describe plans for the recruitment of subjects and the consent procedures to be followed. Include the circumstances under which consent will be sought and obtained, who will seek it, the nature of the information to be provided to prospective subjects, and the method of documenting consent. State if the Institutional Review Board (IRB) has authorized a modification or waiver of the elements of consent or the requirement for documentation of consent.

(4) Describe potential risks (physical, psychological, social, legal, or other) and assess their likelihood and seriousness. Where appropriate, describe alternative treatments and procedures that might be advantageous to the subjects.

(5) Describe the procedures for protecting against or minimizing potential risks, including risks to confidentiality, and assess their likely effectiveness. Where appropriate, discuss provisions for ensuring necessary medical or professional intervention in the event of adverse effects to the subjects. Also, where appropriate, describe the provisions for monitoring the data collected to ensure the safety of the subjects.

(6) Discuss why the risks to subjects are reasonable in relation to the anticipated benefits to subjects and in relation to the importance of the knowledge that may reasonably be expected to result.

II. Information on Research Activities Involving Human Subjects

A. Definitions.

A research activity involves human subjects if the activity is research, as defined in the Department's regulations, and the research activity will involve use of human subjects, as defined in the regulations.

—Is it a research activity?

The ED Regulations for the Protection of Human Subjects, Title 34, Code of Federal Regulations, Part 97, define research as "a systematic investigation, including research development, testing and evaluation, designed to develop or contribute to generalizable knowledge." *If an activity follows a deliberate plan whose purpose is to develop or contribute to generalizable knowledge, such as an exploratory study or the collection of data to test a hypothesis, it is research.* Activities which meet this definition constitute research whether or not they are conducted or supported under a program which is considered research for other purposes. For example, some demonstration and service programs may include research activities.

—Is it a human subject?

The regulations define human subject as "a living individual about whom an investigator (whether professional or student) conducting research obtains (1) data through intervention or interaction with the individual, or (2) identifiable private information." *(1) If an activity involves obtaining information about a living person by manipulating that person or that person's environment, as might occur when a new instructional technique is tested, or by communicating or interacting with the individual, as occurs with surveys and interviews, the definition of human subject is met. (2) If an activity involves obtaining private information about a living person in such a way that the information can be linked to that individual (the identity of the subject is or may be readily determined by the investigator or associated with the information), the definition of human subject is met.* [Private information includes information about behavior that occurs in a context in which an individual can reasonably expect that no observation or recording is taking place, and information which has been provided for specific purposes by an individual and which the individual can reasonably expect will not be made public (for example, a school health record).]

B. Exemptions.

Research activities in which the only involvement of human subjects will be in one or more of the following six categories of *exemptions* are not covered by the regulations:

(1) Research conducted in established or commonly accepted educational settings, involving normal educational practices, such as (a) research on regular and special education instructional strategies, or (b) research on the effectiveness of or the comparison among instructional techniques, curricula, or classroom management methods.

(2) Research involving the use of educational tests (cognitive, diagnostic, aptitude, achievement), survey procedures, interview procedures or observation of public behavior, unless: (a) information obtained is recorded in such a manner that human subjects can be identified, directly or through identifiers linked to the subjects; and (b) any disclosure of the human subjects' responses outside the research could reasonably place the subjects at risk of criminal or civil liability or be damaging to the subjects' financial standing, employability, or reputation. *If the subjects are children, this exemption applies only to research involving educational tests or observations of*

public behavior when the investigator(s) do not participate in the activities being observed. [Children are defined as persons who have not attained the legal age for consent to treatments or procedures involved in the research, under the applicable law or jurisdiction in which the research will be conducted.]

(3) Research involving the use of educational tests (cognitive, diagnostic, aptitude, achievement), survey procedures, interview procedures or observation of public behavior that is not exempt under section (2) above, if the human subjects are elected or appointed public officials or candidates for public office; or federal statute(s) require(s) without exception that the confidentiality of the personally identifiable information will be maintained throughout the research and thereafter.

(4) Research involving the collection or study of existing data, documents, records, pathological specimens, or diagnostic specimens, if these sources are publicly available or if the information is recorded by the investigator in a manner that subjects cannot be identified, directly or through identifiers linked to the subjects.

(5) Research and demonstration projects which are conducted by or subject to the approval of department or agency heads, and which are designed to study, evaluate, or otherwise examine: (a) public benefit or service programs; (b) procedures for obtaining benefits or services under those programs; (c) possible changes in or alternatives to those programs or procedures; or (d) possible changes in methods or levels of payment for benefits or services under those programs.

(6) Taste and food quality evaluation and consumer acceptance studies, (a) if wholesome foods without additives are consumed or (b) if a food is consumed that contains a food ingredient at or below the level and for a use found to be safe, or agricultural chemical or environmental contaminant at or below the level found to be safe, by the Food and Drug Administration or approved by the Environmental Protection Agency or the Food Safety and Inspection Service of the U.S Department of Agriculture.

Copies of the Department of Education's Regulations for the Protection of Human Subjects, 34 CFR Part 97 and other pertinent materials on the protection of human subjects in research are available from the Grants Policy and Oversight Staff (GPOS) Office of the Chief Financial and Chief Information Officer, U.S. Department of Education, Washington, D.C., telephone: (202) 708-8263, and on the U.S. Department of Education's Protection of Human Subjects in Research Web Site at http://ocfo.ed.gov/humansub.htm.

U.S. DEPARTMENT OF EDUCATION
BUDGET INFORMATION
NON-CONSTRUCTION PROGRAMS

OMB Control Number: 1890-0004

Expiration Date: 02/28/2003

Applicants requesting funding for only one year should complete the column under "Project Year 1." Applicants requesting funding for multi-year grants should complete all applicable columns. Please read all instructions before completing form.

Name of Institution/Organization

SECTION A - BUDGET SUMMARY
U.S. DEPARTMENT OF EDUCATION FUNDS

Budget Categories	Project Year 1 (a)	Project Year 2 (b)	Project Year 3 (c)	Project Year 4 (d)	Project Year 5 (e)	Total (f)
1. Personnel						
2. Fringe Benefits						
3. Travel						
4. Equipment						
5. Supplies						
6. Contractual						
7. Construction						
8. Other						
9. Total Direct Costs (lines 1-8)						
10. Indirect Costs						
11. Training Stipends						
12. Total Costs (lines 9-11)						

ED Form No. 524

Name of Institution/Organization

Applicants requesting funding for only one year should complete the column under "Project Year 1." Applicants requesting funding for multi-year grants should complete all applicable columns. Please read all instructions before completing form.

SECTION B - BUDGET SUMMARY
NON-FEDERAL FUNDS

Budget Categories	Project Year 1 (a)	Project Year 2 (b)	Project Year 3 (c)	Project Year 4 (d)	Project Year 5 (e)	Total (f)
1. Personnel						
2. Fringe Benefits						
3. Travel						
4. Equipment						
5. Supplies						
6. Contractual						
7. Construction						
8. Other						
9. Total Direct Costs (lines 1-8)						
10. Indirect Costs						
11. Training Stipends						
12. Total Costs (lines 9-11)						

SECTION C - OTHER BUDGET INFORMATION (see instructions)

ED Form No. 524

121

INSTRUCTIONS FOR ED FORM 524

General Instructions

This form is used to apply to individual U.S. Department of Education discretionary grant programs. Unless directed otherwise, provide the same budget information for each year of the multi-year funding request. Pay attention to applicable program specific instructions, if attached.

Section A - Budget Summary
U.S. Department of Education Funds

All applicants must complete Section A and provide a breakdown by the applicable budget categories shown in lines 1-11.

Lines 1-11, columns (a)-(e): For each project year for which funding is requested, show the total amount requested for each applicable budget category.

Lines 1-11, column (f): Show the multi-year total for each budget category. If funding is requested for only one project year, leave this column blank.

Line 12, columns (a)-(e): Show the total budget request for each project year for which funding is requested.

Line 12, column (f): Show the total amount requested for all project years. If funding is requested for only one year, leave this space blank.

Section B - Budget Summary
Non-Federal Funds

If you are required to provide or volunteer to provide matching funds or other non-Federal resources to the project, these should be shown for each applicable budget category on lines 1-11 of Section B.

Lines 1-11, columns (a)-(e): For each project year for which matching funds or other contributions are provided, show the total

contribution for each applicable budget category.

Lines 1-11, column (f): Show the multi-year total for each budget category. If non-Federal contributions are provided for only one year, leave this column blank.

Line 12, columns (a)-(e): Show the total matching or other contribution for each project year.

Line 12, column (f): Show the total amount to be contributed for all years of the multi-year project. If non-Federal contributions are provided for only one year, leave this space blank.

Section C - Other Budget Information
Pay attention to applicable program specific instructions, if attached.

1. Provide an itemized budget breakdown, by project year, for each budget category listed in Sections A and B.

2. If applicable to this program, enter the type of indirect rate (provisional, predetermined, final or fixed) that will be in effect during the funding period. In addition, enter the estimated amount of the base to which the rate is applied, and the total indirect expense.

3. If applicable to this program, provide the rate and base on which fringe benefits are calculated.

4. Provide other explanations or comments you deem necessary.

OMB Approval No. 0348-0040

ASSURANCES - NON-CONSTRUCTION PROGRAMS

NOTE: Certain of these assurances may not be applicable to your project or program. If you have questions, please contact the awarding agency. Further, certain Federal awarding agencies may require applicants to certify to additional assurances. If such is the case, you will be notified.

As the duly authorized representative of the applicant, I certify that the applicant:

1. Has the legal authority to apply for Federal assistance and the institutional, managerial and financial capability (including funds sufficient to pay the non-Federal share of project cost) to ensure proper planning, management and completion of the project described in this application.

2. Will give the awarding agency, the Comptroller General of the United States and, if appropriate, the State, through any authorized representative, access to and the right to examine all records, books, papers, or documents related to the award; and will establish a proper accounting system in accordance with generally accepted accounting standards or agency directives.

3. Will establish safeguards to prohibit employees from using their positions for a purpose that constitutes or presents the appearance of personal or organizational conflict of interest, or personal gain.

4. Will initiate and complete the work within the applicable time frame after receipt of approval of the awarding agency.

5. Will comply with the Intergovernmental Personnel Act of 1970 (42 U.S.C. §§4728-4763) relating to prescribed standards for merit systems for programs funded under one of the 19 statutes or regulations specified in Appendix A of OPM's Standards for a Merit System of Personnel Administration (5 C.F.R. 900, Subpart F).

6. Will comply with all Federal statutes relating to nondiscrimination. These include but are not limited to: (a) Title VI of the Civil Rights Act of 1964 (P.L. 88-352) which prohibits discrimination on the basis of race, color or national origin; (b) Title IX of the Education Amendments of 1972, as amended (20 U.S.C. §§1681-1683, and 1685-1686), which prohibits discrimination on the basis of sex; (c) Section 504 of the Rehabilitation Act of 1973, as amended (29 U.S.C. §794), which prohibits discrimination on the basis of handicaps; (d) the Age Discrimination Act of 1975, as amended (42 U.S.C. §§6101-6107), which prohibits discrimination on the basis of age; (e) the Drug Abuse Office and Treatment Act of 1972 (P.L. 92-255), as amended, relating to nondiscrimination on the basis of drug abuse; (f) the Comprehensive Alcohol Abuse and Alcoholism Prevention, Treatment and Rehabilitation Act of 1970 (P.L. 91-616), as amended, relating to nondiscrimination on the basis of alcohol abuse or alcoholism; (g) §§523 and 527 of the Public Health Service Act of 1912 (42 U.S.C. §§290 dd-3 and 290 ee 3), as amended, relating to confidentiality of alcohol and drug abuse patient records; (h) Title VIII of the Civil Rights Act of 1968 (42 U.S.C. §§3601 et seq.), as amended, relating to nondiscrimination in the sale, rental or financing of housing; (i) any other nondiscrimination provisions in the specific statute(s) under which application for Federal assistance is being made; and, (j) the requirements of any other nondiscrimination statute(s) which may apply to the application.

7. Will comply, or has already complied, with the requirements of Titles II and III of the Uniform Relocation Assistance and Real Property Acquisition Policies Act of 1970 (P.L. 91-646) which provide for fair and equitable treatment of persons displaced or whose property is acquired as a result of Federal or federally-assisted programs. These requirements apply to all interests in real property acquired for project purposes regardless of Federal participation in purchases.

8. Will comply, as applicable, with provisions of the Hatch Act (5 U.S.C. §§1501-1508 and 7324-7328) which limit the political activities of employees whose principal employment activities are funded in whole or in part with Federal funds.

Previous Edition Usable

Authorized for Local Reproduction

Standard Form 424B (Rev. 7-97)
Prescribed by OMB Circular A-102

9. Will comply, as applicable, with the provisions of the Davis-Bacon Act (40 U.S.C. §§276a to 276a-7), the Copeland Act (40 U.S.C. §276c and 18 U.S.C. §874), and the Contract Work Hours and Safety Standards Act (40 U.S.C. §§327-333), regarding labor standards for federally-assisted construction subagreements.

10. Will comply, if applicable, with flood insurance purchase requirements of Section 102(a) of the Flood Disaster Protection Act of 1973 (P.L. 93-234) which requires recipients in a special flood hazard area to participate in the program and to purchase flood insurance if the total cost of insurable construction and acquisition is $10,000 or more.

11. Will comply with environmental standards which may be prescribed pursuant to the following: (a) institution of environmental quality control measures under the National Environmental Policy Act of 1969 (P.L. 91-190) and Executive Order (EO) 11514; (b) notification of violating facilities pursuant to EO 11738; (c) protection of wetlands pursuant to EO 11990; (d) evaluation of flood hazards in floodplains in accordance with EO 11988; (e) assurance of project consistency with the approved State management program developed under the Coastal Zone Management Act of 1972 (16 U.S.C. §§1451 et seq.); (f) conformity of Federal actions to State (Clean Air) Implementation Plans under Section 176(c) of the Clean Air Act of 1955, as amended (42 U.S.C. §§7401 et seq.); (g) protection of underground sources of drinking water under the Safe Drinking Water Act of 1974, as amended (P.L. 93-523); and, (h) protection of endangered species under the Endangered Species Act of 1973, as amended (P.L. 93-205).

12. Will comply with the Wild and Scenic Rivers Act of 1968 (16 U.S.C. §§1271 et seq.) related to protecting components or potential components of the national wild and scenic rivers system.

13. Will assist the awarding agency in assuring compliance with Section 106 of the National Historic Preservation Act of 1966, as amended (16 U.S.C. §470), EO 11593 (identification and protection of historic properties), and the Archaeological and Historic Preservation Act of 1974 (16 U.S.C. §§469a-1 et seq.).

14. Will comply with P.L. 93-348 regarding the protection of human subjects involved in research, development, and related activities supported by this award of assistance.

15. Will comply with the Laboratory Animal Welfare Act of 1966 (P.L. 89-544, as amended, 7 U.S.C. §§2131 et seq.) pertaining to the care, handling, and treatment of warm blooded animals held for research, teaching, or other activities supported by this award of assistance.

16. Will comply with the Lead-Based Paint Poisoning Prevention Act (42 U.S.C. §§4801 et seq.) which prohibits the use of lead-based paint in construction or rehabilitation of residence structures.

17. Will cause to be performed the required financial and compliance audits in accordance with the Single Audit Act Amendments of 1996 and OMB Circular No. A-133, "Audits of States, Local Governments, and Non-Profit Organizations."

18. Will comply with all applicable requirements of all other Federal laws, executive orders, regulations, and policies governing this program.

SIGNATURE OF AUTHORIZED CERTIFYING OFFICIAL	TITLE
APPLICANT ORGANIZATION	DATE SUBMITTED

Standard Form 424B (Rev. 7-97) Back

CERTIFICATIONS REGARDING LOBBYING; DEBARMENT, SUSPENSION AND OTHER RESPONSIBILITY MATTERS; AND DRUG-FREE WORKPLACE REQUIREMENTS

Applicants should refer to the regulations cited below to determine the certification to which they are required to attest. Applicants should also review the instructions for certification included in the regulations before completing this form. Signature of this form provides for compliance with certification requirements under 34 CFR Part 82, "New Restrictions on Lobbying," and 34 CFR Part 85, "Government-wide Debarment and Suspension (Nonprocurement) and Government-wide Requirements for Drug-Free Workplace (Grants)." The certifications shall be treated as a material representation of fact upon which reliance will be placed when the Department of Education determines to award the covered transaction, grant, or cooperative agreement.

1. LOBBYING

As required by Section 1352, Title 31 of the U.S. Code, and implemented at 34 CFR Part 82, for persons entering into a grant or cooperative agreement over $100,000, as defined at 34 CFR Part 82, Sections 82.105 and 82.110, the applicant certifies that:

(a) No Federal appropriated funds have been paid or will be paid, by or on behalf of the undersigned, to any person for influencing or attempting to influence an officer or employee of any agency, a Member of Congress, an officer or employee of Congress, or an employee of a Member of Congress in connection with the making of any Federal grant, the entering into of any cooperative agreement, and the extension, continuation, renewal, amendment, or modification of any Federal grant or cooperative agreement;

(b) If any funds other than Federal appropriated funds have been paid or will be paid to any person for influencing or attempting to influence an officer or employee of any agency, a Member of Congress, an officer or employee of Congress, or an employee of a Member of Congress in connection with this Federal grant or cooperative agreement, the undersigned shall complete and submit Standard Form - LLL, "Disclosure Form to Report Lobbying," in accordance with its instructions;

(c) The undersigned shall require that the language of this certification be included in the award documents for all subawards at all tiers (including subgrants, contracts under grants and cooperative agreements, and subcontracts) and that all subrecipients shall certify and disclose accordingly.

2. DEBARMENT, SUSPENSION, AND OTHER RESPONSIBILITY MATTERS

As required by Executive Order 12549, Debarment and Suspension, and implemented at 34 CFR Part 85, for prospective participants in primary covered transactions, as defined at 34 CFR Part 85, Sections 85.105 and 85.110—

A. The applicant certifies that it and its principals:

(a) Are not presently debarred, suspended, proposed for debarment, declared ineligible, or voluntarily excluded from covered transactions by any Federal department or agency;

(b) Have not within a three-year period preceding this application been convicted of or had a civil judgement rendered against them for commission of fraud or a criminal offense in connection with obtaining, attempting to obtain, or performing a public (Federal, State, or local) transaction or contract under a public transaction; violation of Federal or State antitrust statutes or commission of embezzlement, theft, forgery, bribery, falsification or destruction of records, making false statements, or receiving stolen property;

(c) Are not presently indicted for or otherwise criminally or civilly charged by a governmental entity (Federal, State, or local) with commission of any of the offenses enumerated in paragraph (2)(b) of this certification; and

(d) Have not within a three-year period preceding this application had one or more public transaction (Federal, State, or local) terminated for cause or default; and

B. Where the applicant is unable to certify to any of the statements in this certification, he or she shall attach an explanation to this application.

3. DRUG-FREE WORKPLACE (GRANTEES OTHER THAN INDIVIDUALS)

As required by the Drug-Free Workplace Act of 1988, and implemented at 34 CFR Part 85, Subpart F, for grantees, as defined at 34 CFR Part 85, Sections 85.605 and 85.610 -

A. The applicant certifies that it will or will continue to provide a drug-free workplace by:

(a) Publishing a statement notifying employees that the unlawful manufacture, distribution, dispensing, possession, or use of a controlled substance is prohibited in the grantee's workplace and specifying the actions that will be taken against employees for violation of such prohibition;

(b) Establishing an on-going drug-free awareness program to inform employees about:

(1) The dangers of drug abuse in the workplace;

(2) The grantee's policy of maintaining a drug-free workplace;

(3) Any available drug counseling, rehabilitation, and employee assistance programs; and

(4) The penalties that may be imposed upon employees for drug abuse violations occurring in the workplace;

(c) Making it a requirement that each employee to be engaged in the performance of the grant be given a copy of the statement required by paragraph (a);

(d) Notifying the employee in the statement required by paragraph (a) that, as a condition of employment under the grant, the employee will:

(1) Abide by the terms of the statement; and

(2) Notify the employer in writing of his or her conviction for a violation of a criminal drug statute occurring in the workplace no later than five calendar days after such conviction;

(e) Notifying the agency, in writing, within 10 calendar days after receiving notice under subparagraph (d)(2) from an employee or otherwise receiving actual notice of such conviction. Employers of convicted employees must provide notice, including position title, to: Director, Grants Policy and Oversight Staff, U.S. Department of Education, 400 Maryland Avenue, S.W. (Room 3652, GSA Regional Office Building No. 3), Washington, DC 20202-4248. Notice shall include the identification number(s) of each affected grant;

(f) Taking one of the following actions, within 30 calendar days of receiving notice under subparagraph (d)(2), with respect to any employee who is so convicted:

(1) Taking appropriate personnel action against such an employee, up to and including termination, consistent with the requirements of the Rehabilitation Act of 1973, as amended; or

(2) Requiring such employee to participate satisfactorily in a drug abuse assistance or rehabilitation program approved for such purposes by a Federal, State, or local health, law enforcement, or other appropriate agency;

(g) Making a good faith effort to continue to maintain a drug-free workplace through implementation of paragraphs (a), (b), (c), (d), (e), and (f).

B. The grantee may insert in the space provided below the site(s) for the performance of work done in connection with the specific grant:

Place of Performance (Street address. city, county, state, zip code)

_____

_____

_____

Check **[ ]** if there are workplaces on file that are not identified here.

_____

**DRUG-FREE WORKPLACE
(GRANTEES WHO ARE INDIVIDUALS)**

As required by the Drug-Free Workplace Act of 1988, and implemented at 34 CFR Part 85, Subpart F, for grantees. as defined at 34 CFR Part 85, Sections 85.605 and 85.610-

A. As a condition of the grant, I certify that I will not engage in the unlawful manufacture, distribution, dispensing, possession, or use of a controlled substance in conducting any activity with the grant; and

B. If convicted of a criminal drug offense resulting from a violation occurring during the conduct of any grant activity, I will report the conviction, in writing, within 10 calendar days of the conviction, to: Director, Grants Policy and Oversight Staff, Department of Education, 400 Maryland Avenue, S.W. (Room 3652, GSA Regional Office Building No. 3), Washington, DC 20202-4248. Notice shall include the identification number(s) of each affected grant.

As the duly authorized representative of the applicant, I hereby certify that the applicant will comply with the above certifications.

NAME OF APPLICANT	PR/AWARD NUMBER AND / OR PROJECT NAME
PRINTED NAME AND TITLE OF AUTHORIZED REPRESENTATIVE	
SIGNATURE	DATE

ED 80-0013

12/98

Certification Regarding Debarment, Suspension, Ineligibility and Voluntary Exclusion — Lower Tier Covered Transactions

This certification is required by the Department of Education regulations implementing Executive Order 12549, Debarment and Suspension, 34 CFR Part 85, for all lower tier transactions meeting the threshold and tier requirements stated at Section 85.110.

Instructions for Certification

1. By signing and submitting this proposal, the prospective lower tier participant is providing the certification set out below.

2. The certification in this clause is a material representation of fact upon which reliance was placed when this transaction was entered into. If it is later determined that the prospective lower tier participant knowingly rendered an erroneous certification, in addition to other remedies available to the Federal Government, the department or agency with which this transaction originated may pursue available remedies, including suspension and/or debarment.

3. The prospective lower tier participant shall provide immediate written notice to the person to which this proposal is submitted if at any time the prospective lower tier participant learns that its certification was erroneous when submitted or has become erroneous by reason of changed circumstances.

4. The terms "covered transaction," "debarred," "suspended," "ineligible," "lower tier covered transaction," "participant," " person," "primary covered transaction," " principal," "proposal," and "voluntarily excluded," as used in this clause, have the meanings set out in the Definitions and Coverage sections of rules implementing Executive Order 12549. You may contact the person to which this proposal is submitted for assistance in obtaining a copy of those regulations.

5. The prospective lower tier participant agrees by submitting this proposal that, should the proposed covered transaction be entered into, it shall not knowingly enter into any lower tier covered transaction with a person who is debarred, suspended, declared ineligible, or voluntarily excluded from participation in this covered transaction, unless authorized by the department or agency with which this transaction originated.

6. The prospective lower tier participant further agrees by submitting this proposal that it will include the clause titled "Certification Regarding Debarment, Suspension, Ineligibility, and Voluntary Exclusion-Lower Tier Covered Transactions," without modification, in all lower tier covered transactions and in all solicitations for lower tier covered transactions.

7. A participant in a covered transaction may rely upon a certification of a prospective participant in a lower tier covered transaction that it is not debarred, suspended, ineligible, or voluntarily excluded from the covered transaction, unless it knows that the certification is erroneous. A participant may decide the method and frequency by which it determines the eligibility of its principals. Each participant may but is not required to, check the Nonprocurement List.

8. Nothing contained in the foregoing shall be construed to require establishment of a system of records in order to render in good faith the certification required by this clause. The knowledge and information of a participant is not required to exceed that which is normally possessed by a prudent person in the ordinary course of business dealings.

9. Except for transactions authorized under paragraph 5 of these instructions, if a participant in a covered transaction knowingly enters into a lower tier covered transaction with a person who is suspended, debarred, ineligible, or voluntarily excluded from participation in this transaction, in addition to other remedies available to the Federal Government, the department or agency with which this transaction originated may pursue available remedies, including suspension and/or debarment.

Certification

(1)   The prospective lower tier participant certifies, by submission of this proposal, that neither it nor its principals are presently debarred, suspended, proposed for debarment, declared ineligible, or voluntarily excluded from participation in this transaction by any Federal department or agency.

(2)   Where the prospective lower tier participant is unable to certify to any of the statements in this certification, such prospective participant shall attach an explanation to this proposal.

NAME OF APPLICANT	PR/AWARD NUMBER AND/OR PROJECT NAME
PRINTED NAME AND TITLE OF AUTHORIZED REPRESENTATIVE	
SIGNATURE	DATE

ED 80-0014, 9/90 (Replaces GCS-009 (REV.12/88), which is obsolete)

DISCLOSURE OF LOBBYING ACTIVITIES

Complete this form to disclose lobbying activities pursuant to 31 U.S.C. 1352
(See reverse for public burden disclosure.)

Approved by OMB
0348-0046

1. Type of Federal Action:	2. Status of Federal Action:	3. Report Type:
⬚ a. contract ⬚ b. grant c. cooperative agreement d. loan e. loan guarantee f. loan insurance	⬚ a. bid/offer/application ⬚ b. initial award c. post-award	⬚ a. initial filing ⬚ b. material change **For Material Change Only:** year _____ quarter _____ date of last report _____

4. Name and Address of Reporting Entity: ☐ Prime ☐ Subawardee Tier _____, *if known*: Congressional District, *if known*:	5. If Reporting Entity in No. 4 is a Subawardee, Enter Name and Address of Prime: Congressional District, *if known*:
6. Federal Department/Agency:	7. Federal Program Name/Description: CFDA Number, *if applicable*: _____
8. Federal Action Number, *if known*:	9. Award Amount, *if known*: $
10. a. Name and Address of Lobbying Registrant (*if individual, last name, first name, MI*):	b. Individuals Performing Services (*including address if different from No. 10a*) (*last name, first name, MI*):

11.	
Information requested through this form is authorized by title 31 U.S.C. section 1352. This disclosure of lobbying activities is a material representation of fact upon which reliance was placed by the tier above when this transaction was made or entered into. This disclosure is required pursuant to 31 U.S.C. 1352. This information will be reported to the Congress semi-annually and will be available for public inspection. Any person who fails to file the required disclosure shall be subject to a civil penalty of not less that $10,000 and not more than $100,000 for each such failure.	Signature: _____ Print Name: _____ Title: _____ Telephone No.: _____ Date: _____

Federal Use Only:	Authorized for Local Reproduction Standard Form LLL (Rev. 7-97)

INSTRUCTIONS FOR COMPLETION OF SF-LLL, DISCLOSURE OF LOBBYING ACTIVITIES

This disclosure form shall be completed by the reporting entity, whether subawardee or prime Federal recipient, at the initiation or receipt of a covered Federal action, or a material change to a previous filing, pursuant to title 31 U.S.C. section 1352. The filing of a form is required for each payment or agreement to make payment to any lobbying entity for influencing or attempting to influence an officer or employee of any agency, a Member of Congress, an officer or employee of Congress, or an employee of a Member of Congress in connection with a covered Federal action. Complete all items that apply for both the initial filing and material change report. Refer to the implementing guidance published by the Office of Management and Budget for additional information.

1. Identify the type of covered Federal action for which lobbying activity is and/or has been secured to influence the outcome of a covered Federal action.

2. Identify the status of the covered Federal action.

3. Identify the appropriate classification of this report. If this is a followup report caused by a material change to the information previously reported, enter the year and quarter in which the change occurred. Enter the date of the last previously submitted report by this reporting entity for this covered Federal action.

4. Enter the full name, address, city, State and zip code of the reporting entity. Include Congressional District, if known. Check the appropriate classification of the reporting entity that designates if it is, or expects to be, a prime or subaward recipient. Identify the tier of the subawardee, e.g., the first subawardee of the prime is the 1st tier. Subawards include but are not limited to subcontracts, subgrants and contract awards under grants.

5. If the organization filing the report in item 4 checks "Subawardee," then enter the full name, address, city, State and zip code of the prime Federal recipient. Include Congressional District, if known.

6. Enter the name of the Federal agency making the award or loan commitment. Include at least one organizational level below agency name, if known. For example, Department of Transportation, United States Coast Guard.

7. Enter the Federal program name or description for the covered Federal action (item 1). If known, enter the full Catalog of Federal Domestic Assistance (CFDA) number for grants, cooperative agreements, loans, and loan commitments.

8. Enter the most appropriate Federal identifying number available for the Federal action identified in item 1 (e.g., Request for Proposal (RFP) number; Invitation for Bid (IFB) number; grant announcement number; the contract, grant, or loan award number; the application/proposal control number assigned by the Federal agency). Include prefixes, e.g., "RFP-DE-90-001."

9. For a covered Federal action where there has been an award or loan commitment by the Federal agency, enter the Federal amount of the award/loan commitment for the prime entity identified in item 4 or 5.

10. (a) Enter the full name, address, city, State and zip code of the lobbying registrant under the Lobbying Disclosure Act of 1995 engaged by the reporting entity identified in item 4 to influence the covered Federal action.

    (b) Enter the full names of the individual(s) performing services, and include full address if different from 10 (a). Enter Last Name, First Name, and Middle Initial (MI).

11. The certifying official shall sign and date the form, print his/her name, title, and telephone number.

References

Allison, K. R., Silverman, G., & Dignam, C. (1990). Effects on students of teacher training in use of a drug education curriculum. *Journal of Drug Education 20*(1), 31–46.

American Psychological Association. (1994). *Publication manual of the American Psychological Association* (4th ed.). Washington, DC: Author.

Brewer, E., Achilles, C. M., & Fuhriman, J. R. (1998). *Finding funding: Grantwriting from start to finish, including project management and Internet use.* Thousand Oaks, CA: Corwin.

Connell, D. B., Turner, R. R., & Mason, E. F. (1985, October). Summary of findings of the school health education evaluation: Health promotion effectiveness, implementation, and costs. *Journal of School Health, 55*(8), 316–321.

Knowles, C. R. (1993, September-October). Confessions of a Grant Writer. *Student Assistance Journal,* pp.33-34.

Reviewing applications for discretionary grants and cooperative agreements: A workbook for application reviewers [Training Manual]. (1991, October). Washington, DC: Horace Mann Learning Center, U.S. Department of Education.

Sherman, L. W., Gottfredson, D., MacKenzie, D., Eck, J., Reuter, P., & Bushway, S. (1997). *Preventing crime: What works, what doesn't, what's promising.* College Park, MD: U.S. Department of Justice, Office of Justice Programs.

Other Grantwriting Resources

Blum, Laurie. (1996). *The complete guide to getting a grant: How to turn your ideas into dollars.* New York: John Wiley.

Brewer, Ernest W., Achilles, Charles M., & Fuhriman, Jay R. (2001). *Finding funding: Grantwriting from start to finish, including project management and Internet use.* Thousand Oaks, CA: Corwin.

Browning, Beverly. (2001). *Grant Writing for Dummies.* New York: Hungry Minds.

Burke, Jim, & Prater, Carol Ann. (2000). *I'll grant you that: A step-by-step guide to finding funds, designing winning projects, and writing powerful proposals* [Book and CD-ROM]. Portsmouth, NH: Heinemann.

Carlson, Mim. (1995). *Winning grants step by step: Support centers of America's complete workbook for planning, developing and writing successful proposals.* San Francisco: Jossey-Bass.

Gitlin, Laura N., & Lyons, Kevin J. (1996). *Successful grant writing: Strategies for health and human service professionals.* New York: Springer.

Golden, Susan. (1997). *Secrets of successful grantsmanship: A guerrilla guide to raising money.* San Francisco: Jossey-Bass.

Hall, Mary S. (1988). *Getting funded: A complete guide to proposal writing* (3rd ed.). Portland, OR: Continuing Education Press.

Hoffman, Don, Lamoreaux, Denise, & Hayes, Lisa (Eds.). (1999). *Winning strategies for developing grant proposals.* Washington, DC: Thompson.

McIlnay, Dennis P., & McIlnay, Dennis A. *How foundations work: What grantseekers need to know about the many faces of foundations* (Nonprofit and Public Management Series). San Francisco: Jossey-Bass.

Miller, Patrick. (2000). *Grant writing: Strategies for developing winning proposals.* Miller and Associates.

New, Cheryl Carter, & Quick, James Aaron. (1998). *Grantseeker's toolkit: A comprehensive guide to finding funding* (Non-Profit Law, Finance, and Management Series). New York: John Wiley.

Orlich, Donald C. (1996). *Designing successful grant proposals.* Alexandria, VA: ASCD.

Miner, Lynn E., Miner, Jeremy T., & Griffith, Jerry. (1998). *Proposal planning and writing* (2nd ed.). Phoenix, AZ: Oryx Press.

Reif-Lehrer, Liane. (1995). *Grant application writers handbook.* Boston: Jones-Bartlett.

U.S. Department of Education. (1995). *What should I know about ED grants?* Washington, DC: Author.

Index

CORWIN
PRESS

The Corwin Press logo—a raven striding across an open book—represents the happy union of courage and learning. We are a professional-level publisher of books and journals for K-12 educators, and we are committed to creating and providing resources that embody these qualities. Corwin's motto is "Success for All Learners."